MW00748025

ON THE OKEY DOKEY TRAIL

A SMART-ALECK PERSPECTIVE ON THE GIVE AND TAKE OF LIFE

I. LEIGH PRIVATE

BIF Press

ON THE OKEY DOKEY TRAIL: A SMART-ALECK PERSPECTIVE
ON THE GIVE AND TAKE OF LIFE

BIF Press

Copyright © 2014 by I. Leigh Private

Published in the United States of America.

Author website: www.ileighprivate.com
and www.ontheokeydokeytrail.com

TABLE OF CONTENTS

About Me

After reading this book, please place adjectives here:

PREFACE

I think we were about eight years old when our mother sat down at the upright piano at our grandmother's house and revealed an unknown part of herself to us. I can still see the look on my twin brother's face and feel that strange sense of shock mixed with awe when she began to play (I am now certain of the origin of *shock and awe*, "W" must have known our mother). There would be no *chopsticks* for her; she played a Rachmaninoff piano concerto. It was a stunning performance. When it was over she simply closed the piano and proceeded to go about her business as if nothing out of the ordinary had just occurred. Later in the day, we learned from our grandmother that our mother had been a concert pianist trained at The Toronto Conservatory of Music.

Our mother was so secretive about her life and her past that we thought maybe she was a spy. Since we grew up in the James Bond Cold War era, all that spy stuff seemed plausible and provided endless entertainment as we imagined her tangling with the KGB. No doubt, she was payback for all of those pogroms. Over the years, despite our repeated interrogations, our mother gave us very little information about herself. We had a name and rank, mother, but no serial number. That day, and the music from it, motivated this opus.

Like my mother, I had kids late in life. Unlike my mother, I want my kids to know me and to see me as more than their mother. I want them to see me, like themselves, as just another human being feeling her way through life. And since there seems to be no escape from the inheritance of traits and aspects of personality from one generation to the next, I thought it would be fun to give my kids a preview of what's to come . . . poor little bastards.

I did have issues to surmount: a more than fifty-year case of writer's block, abject fear, and various other bullshit excuses. My biggest issue: while I don't consider myself *spy material* like my mommy, I am, and have always been, private—intensely. Because of this, and because guessing games are just so much fun, I have chosen to keep most identities concealed (including my own), and I have been thoughtfully selective about the stories to share (I have teenage daughters). Do names really matter anyway? What am I talking about; it's fun to dish from time to time. One of my favorite jokes is from Drew Carey. He told it to me while he was sitting in my office years before his hit sitcom: "Don't name drop. My friend Bobby De Niro told me that."

Since I worked in the *entertainment business* for many years, and with this I mean television production, not pole-dancing, exceptions to the *name drop rule* will be made. I will use these exceptions only when the memory doesn't violate anyone's privacy or the implicit trust that professional courtesy demands, or, as long as it isn't too terribly nasty.

Now, back to secrets: a friend once commented, "The secret to life is to die without having one." Easier said than done, buster. Anyway, this will be a start. The following stories are little slivers of a life. They are designed to stand alone, but somehow fit together. A warning: should you choose to read further, you will follow a bouncing ball in time. My brain was once described as a pinball machine, so the order or chaos herein is unavoidable. One last preface, while I did have this opus copy-edited for screaming spelling and grammatical mistakes, I have no interest in making it *perfect*. Were that to be the case, this piece would be totally unrecognizable to my friends, family, and self.

My key players

My Twin:
A larger than life character that left life too soon.
He is profoundly missed.

My Husband:
After a few weeks together he astutely observed, "You don't need a boyfriend, you need a manager."

Over the years, he has repeatedly mentioned that without him I'd be sitting on boxes in my college apartment trying to pack while using tweezers* to eat SpaghettiO's from out of a half-opened can.

(*It was a fork)

I am eternally grateful for his help in packing and generally in moving me forward.

My Two Daughters:

Without whom my life would have been a miss.

LOSING YOUR CURRENCY

To celebrate my fiftieth birthday, my fourteen-year-old daughter and I went on a hiking tour of Bhutan. I had always wanted to go there since having learned about this far away magical kingdom thirty years earlier while researching a documentary. We were now in a place where *Gross National Happiness* was the standard measure by which the country accessed its wealth. I was looking forward to emptying my mind in the land of blissful happiness while commemorating my half-century milestone.

It started out well. I had been telling everyone I came in contact with: the tour guides, the bus driver, shopkeepers, monks, and farmers, who spoke no English, that I was there celebrating my fiftieth year on the planet. I was met with smiles, knowing nods, and maybe a few eye rolls. I thought of my half-century mark as an auspicious accomplishment. It had not taken long before I began to go native; using the word *auspicious* was the first sign.

One of the women on our trip, probably having grown

sick of hearing all this birthday chatter, stopped me on a hike one day and remarked, "If I were you, I'd shut up about being fifty, it's around the age where women start to *disappear* and lose their *currency*. Huh? Women disappearing? This was not the kind of magic I expected to hear about in the land of the truly happy. Was this a Bhutan thing? Did she mean that I should stop talking about it while in the mountains? There was a lot of silence going on around there.

It occurred to me that the first three letters of the sacred mountain range we were in was *HIM*. Just a coincidence, I assumed, never mind that all of the houses there had phallic signs on them. Back to *currency* . . . what exactly did she mean? I thought about actual currency, as in money. I was pretty sure there were only men on all the bills I had ever seen. Come to think of it, paper money was given a man's name: *Bill*. Maybe I was on to something. Wait, wasn't The Queen of England on the pound? Of course, it would have to refer to weight, ugh. I started to think of all the women that should be on *bills*, currency, bank notes, whatever: Mother Theresa, Indira Gandhi, Ruth Gordon, Kristen, Tina, Amy, Ellen, Teri, Gilda, Bette, Lily, Lucy— the list would be long.

I ran back to the woman who had so confused me on our morning hike. "Um, excuse me, I'm missing something here, or maybe it's the altitude, but I haven't a clue about what you actually mean."

"Fifty is around the time when women cease to be

visible, valuable or attractive to the opposite sex, I thought you were smarter . . . this is the cliff," she incredulously responded. Cliffs mattered here and we were warned to avoid them. She went on to tell me about the fateful moment when she herself made this discovery: she was at a dinner party seated next to a man whom she did not know. He was attractive and attentive; the banter between them, while not reaching the *Nick and Nora* level, was fun and amusing UNTIL . . . she happened to mention her recent celebration of her fiftieth birthday. He then turned away and all but ignored her for the rest of that evening. "Well, maybe he was just an asshole," I was trying to make her, and myself, feel better. "Yes, but he was not the only one and this was not the only time."

She continued to explain: "The girl voodoo, that je ne sais quoi effect, the power women possess as it relates to men, seriously degrades around that time of life." Degrades? Wait, what was that symbol on the period chart? Was there really a half-life for women's attractiveness to the opposite sex? I had not seriously considered any of this during my recent birthday celebration and announcement to well, everyone I had ever met.

But wait . . . hold the presses! My grandmother got married, for her third time, **in her seventies**. That flies in the face of all this. My mind was spinning. I began to search through my cerebral file cabinet looking for anything that might help me make sense of all this. I was on high-skim searching the files of the great thinkers and truth tellers I had studied until I came upon the work of that wise sage, Samantha, from "Sex in the City." In the episode where Samantha discovered a strand of gray in her pubic hair, she declared, "Nobody wants to fuck grandma's pussy!" BUT WAIT, I have evidence to the contrary!

Leaving my fourteen-year-old daughter out of this debate, I went around to the other older women on the tour to discuss this topic and gain some additional insight. I seemed to be annoying to a few during their time and place of peaceful repose, but consensus did reluctantly emerge. This was, in fact, *a truth;* something one might be able to take to the bank. Not wanting to take anything at face value, and always up for an experiment, I was determined to test this thesis upon my return home. I was on it like red on rice.

Since I had just returned from a place that nobody had ever heard of, I thought I would be prime guest material to have at someone's dinner party. This would be my very own little petri dish. I began to look through my email to connect with people who were likely to be having dinner parties with other guests who would not know me. I needed to be scientific about this. Within a few days I had insinuated myself into several upcoming events; the trials would begin. My husband was neither enthusiastic about attending any of these events, nor did he see the value of the mission. I think he was tiring of my *stupid antics*. Aha! And so it begins.

I approached my first party with breathless anticipation.

Truly, I had never seen so many steps up to someone's front door. I was a little nervous and sweating like a pig by the time I crossed the threshold. Mercifully, I was never without a fresh drink in my hand, which was provided by the cute young bartender. I started to relax. It was a fun crowd and there were a couple of very attractive men around my age in attendance. As luck would have it, I was seated next to the gentleman who most especially caught my eye.

It was time to ramp up the charm and pray that no salad got lodged in my teeth. It didn't take long before we were completely engaged like a four-alarm fire. It was so much fun and quite reinforcing to my initial hypothesis. What was that woman talking about? I saw no real evidence of my currency being devalued. As I was feeling smug and a bit tipsy, my handsome lab rat began to talk about his partner who happened to be sitting down at the other end of the table. Partner? Did he say partner? They were a couple? My trial subject was gay. I am so dense. This experiment was a total disqualification and had to be thrown out. Nevertheless, it was a wonderful party. My man was totally charming and delightful . . . as was his partner.

After this first soiree, I began to rethink the dinner party strategy. Not only were there too many calories involved, but also the high heels were in serious conflict with my feet.

I would try and move this experiment into my exciting everyday life instead. Before setting out to the grocery store, which had many times been a source of positive reinforcement generating both good feelings and dinner, I dug

11

out some pictures of myself to inspect from my twenties. I didn't think of myself that differently from before; I was still the adventurous and carefree (stupid and immature) person I had always been, and I thought I looked about the same, especially if I squinted hard enough.

Off I went to Bob's Market, one of the last independent grocers in LA. They have a great meat and poultry section. I stood on line and waited my turn. I started to recall some of my previous exchanges with the butcher. He was always cheerful and pleasant. "Would you like a rub?" I began to wonder . . . was he really just referring to the tri-tip? Ok, focus. I smiled and went into my very best *girl-flirt* mode when number was called. It was not my usual guy waiting on me. My new man was, however, friendly enough. Then, when I was finished ordering, he spun me around like a test tube in a centrifuge: "Would you like anything else, ma'am?" Ma'am! Just kill me now! Go ahead, take that fucking knife and just kill me now. Why couldn't he have just said, "Miss, sweetie, honey," something that earlier in life I would have found condescending or annoying? Tilt. Game over. There would be no more science experiments.

I couldn't sleep that night. I had a nightmare where a giant syringe filled with fat cells removed from my ass was being pushed into my face to replace the collagen gone missin' by a smirking doctor who looked a lot like the scary Jack Nicholson from *The Shining,* not the cute one from *As Good As It Gets.* I got up and splashed cold water on my face. I did not want to travel down that path. I needed to compose myself.

I closed my eyes and Google-earthed my mind back to

Bhutan. I thought of our destination at the end of that infamous conversation. We had hiked to a beautiful and peaceful monastery, a Buddhist nunnery. I bet all of those women slept soundly even in the *Him*alayan Mountains and I'm sure none of them had any reservations over the number of candles placed in their birthday cake each year. I was then in a more mindful and serene place.

When it comes to the legal tender . . . in G-d We Trust. Happy Birthday.

IT'S A DOUBLEMINT WORLD

Imagine being wheeled into the delivery room only minutes before the doctor was to hit you over the head to deliver your baby (it was common practice in the 1950s to put women under to deliver), and a cocky young intern comes by with a stethoscope in hand, plants it on your belly, then confidently declares, "I hear two heartbeats." This describes the moment our parents found out they would be going home with two—two babies in one pregnancy.

Our mother was forty-one years old when she had us. Because of her age, she was considered *high risk*. She had *one of the very best doctors in New York City*. He was so good that he had no idea she had two babies kicking around. He claimed that he had only ever heard one heartbeat, that *our heartbeats were in sync*. He got that right. Despite this minor oversight, our mother held him in high regard; my middle name was given to me in his honor. When we were born, we were very small, and because of this, we spent the first month or so in a toaster oven being cared for by some *very nice people*. Our parents visited us almost daily.

Unlike the *Doublemint Twins* who were introduced to the world two years before us, we were fraternal twins. I was always surprised when people would ask, "Are you identical or fraternal?" I'd politely answer while thinking: "If one is a boy and the other a girl, they cannot be identical you dumb ass." In terms of birth order, I went first. If you knew my brother, this made complete sense. While I can't be certain, I imagine that our in-utero exit conversation went something like this: "You go ahead and let me know if there is anything worth seeing." He must have been curious, or maybe he just missed me, he followed me a minute later.

Our parents divorced shortly afterward. Something we said? They were married less than two years. It's hard to imagine how they ever got together since they were so different, but luckily for my brother and I, they did. We lived with our mom and saw our father on most Sundays after we were three or four. I can't say that our mom was exactly, or anything like, June Cleaver. Under the circumstances, it was good that my brother and I had each other to help better understand and respond to a parent who was less than perfect (Disclaimer: Our mother loved us but she was a tad complicated). It was also great to have a constant companion and playmate.

We did have other friends, most notably another set of twins, fraternal boys. We spent a lot of happy and quality time together in parks, playgrounds, and dumps. Our favorite place to play was a junkyard located not far from where we lived. We were amazed by what we found there: old radios, vacuum cleaners, and other sundry electronic and mechanical devices. Often, and much to our mother's dismay, we'd bring home some of these treasures to carefully examine before taking them apart. The boys were much more adept at figuring out how things fit back together, but I was equally competent in taking things apart. My brother's goal was to find something that he could repair. He did this once with a vacuum cleaner. He got it to work, but only for a few moments before it fell silent again. It was the *Miracle on Kissena Blvd* that only he and I witnessed and, with the exception of our twin friends, no one else believed.

We also had many early adventures while in New York City. Our grandmother had a bad heart and was in the hospital, the same one where we were born. Hospital rules would not allow us to visit our grandmother with our mother, so we spent hours roaming in what seemed like a vast labyrinth of dark halls in the basement and on the first floor. This is where we encountered our first real life scary monsters . . . we later found out they were Hassidic Jews. We spent all of our time there making up stories about them and hiding in storage rooms and phone booths to escape their capture.

We had curious little minds and active imaginations, and, while most around us didn't share an interest in our *Imagineering*, we constantly bounced ideas off of each other. Our mother had a terrible sense of direction. We thought it was normal to stop at every gas station to ask for directions to get to wherever the hell we were going. That's how everyone drove, right? This got us thinking: what if we could build a guidance system where markers embedded in sidewalk curbs could direct cars to where they needed to go? I wouldn't want you to think we were complete weird-ass nerds; we also talked about how to put an ice-cream machine in our car. We had secret clubs where only we could belong and built forts that only we could enter.

Our mother wanted us to have an early appreciation for the world's greatest treasures and works of art. For years, starting when we were five or six, she'd drop us off at the Metropolitan Museum of Art and later at other fine museums in New York City. I think she needed a time out. We thought this was great and loved the independence we felt and the adventures we had. We imagined ourselves traveling through other times all courtesy of the museum's exhibits; we were cowboys, armored soldiers, and Greek gods. Only once did it get scary when I lost my brother, for what seemed like an eternity, playing hide and seek within the dozens of rooms of Egyptian artifacts. At the end of each day spent there, we'd sit on the cool marble steps in front of the museum with the sun setting behind us, and we'd share a pretzel as we patiently waited for our mom to arrive and take us home.

Like most first generation TV kids, my brother and I loved the tube. Not many kids watched as much news as we did, but we were all on the same page when it came to our love of *The Adventures of Superman*. Our mother liked to put us to bed early. The Man of Steel came on at six thirty each night. The news was on at six. At about five thirty we would start our little routine hoping to convince our mother to let us stay up citing the importance of the news and of us being informed with current events.

The news was often difficult to comprehend, but even more so on Friday nights when the body count from the Vietnam War was tallied. After getting through the news, we'd beg and whine to stay up the extra half hour to watch the latest adventures of our superhero. Truth, justice, and the American way seemed much simpler for Superman than it did for the President and most of the other adults involved with the war.

Our mother's bedroom was a small room off the kitchen. That's where the TV lived. She was asleep the morning of President Kennedy's funeral. We wanted to watch it. We slowly and carefully inched the TV around, on its stand, to an angle so we could view the funeral and not wake her. We sat together on the floor and watched and waited for an adult who could offer a reasonable explanation for what had occurred and to see if the president's kids were ok.

My brother and I both liked President Johnson; in fact, I was an active supporter of his and wrote in chalk on the sidewalks around our apartment complex, *LBJ for the VSA*. For some reason I had a hard time writing the letter *U*. This was one of the first clues to what was to become a big *early in life* struggle. I put together letters the same way I put together disassembled radios, badly. Apparently, our building superintendent did not share my enthusiasm for LBJ. He was very unhappy and made me wash all of the areas I marked. While my brother wasn't a party to this *crime*, he did help me clean up my *mistake*. We thought it was pretty funny.

A few weeks later, we waited with our grandmother on the corner of E. Thirty-Seventh Street in NYC to see LBJ's motorcade emerge from the Midtown Tunnel. We were all excited to catch a glimpse of him. He drove by in an ambulance (it must have been bullet proof) waving as he passed. I remember thinking that he looked old and so small crammed into that car.

As was customary for the time, twins were separated while in school. This created a game-like opportunity where we'd look to find each other, and then we'd figure out our own plan of how best to occupy our time. Our little custom brought our mother to school on many occasions. She was not as happy to see us, as we were to see her.

Generally, school didn't hold much interest for either of us. We both felt out of place there, but for different reasons. My brother was reading way above grade level; I was reading way below. School didn't do much to make accommodations for either one of us. He spent a lot of time sitting outside his class when he was bored and I spent a lot of time *day dreaming* and generally asking too many questions—many of which were apparently off subject. I was as disappointed in my teachers as they were of me. While neither of us were big fans of school (with the exceptions of recess and lunch) we were open minded and hopeful of getting more out of the following year, second grade.

Although my brother was half my size and weight (until he wasn't) he was always very protective of me. I was protective of him as well, but in a different way. The first demonstration of his shielding me from harm was in our apartment playground when some other kids became angry because of something I said or did and wanted to kick the shit out of me. My brother stood nose to nose between the stupid evildoers and me until they backed off and retreated—and all of this without a red cape.

The adult world seemed like it was always in trouble and in constant need of Superman. In our world the thing that mattered most to both of us was both of us. Together, everything made sense and was usually funny; this is how we grew up. The only area where we were ever competitive was in making each other laugh (he'd always win). In our *Doublemint* world, two was always better than one.

ON GETTING
BY AND AROUND

I like to walk, always have. I used to refer to this as *roaming*, but the wireless communication industry has made this term impossible for me to now use. I like the pace, I've found that it lets you see and experience so much more then traveling by other means. Today I took 14,772 steps or walked for 6.36 miles. I know this because of my Fitbit. I hadn't planned on taking all of these steps, not by a long shot.

I was at the beach for my ritual Sunday walk moving faster than traffic on the 405. It was one of those legendary sky-blue sunny LA days. This is not a story about why people hate and love living in LA. This story is about CAR KARMA; I think I have bad Car Karma.

Having finished my walk and only steps from my car, I realized I no longer had my car key. I had detached it from the rest of my keys when I started on my journey. I like to travel light: my key, my iPhone, and the millions of thoughts and voices that course through my head. The missing key was one of those that would likely cost hundreds of dollars to replace. Damn, damn, damn, I was in such a good mood.

Where did I drop that key? How will I find it? How will I start my car? The next question was the most difficult: How was I going to explain it? The *key* might be *the last straw* for my driving and for my marriage. What were the chances of finding it: 1000 to 1? I weighed this against the odds of my husband wanting a divorce after this news: 10 to 1? Did I really want to go look for it? I imagined my younger daughter talking to her friends about her broken home all *seemingly* over a lost key. This long walk back gave me time to reflect on my lifetime of bad Car Karma:

My *auto*biography started out pretty well with me inheriting my first car from my high school boyfriend when he left for college. The car was a Buick LeSabre with a lot of mileage but, most importantly to me, it had a great eight-track cassette player with fantastic speakers and it got me around.

The first time I was stopped by a police officer could have easily been my last. A friend and I decided to pick up another friend to bring her home from *Camp Out In the Middle of Fucking Nowhere*. I don't think that's what it was called . . . it had an Indian name. I was driving her car, Ned the Nova. While I can't recall why it was named Ned, I vividly remember that the car had a particular flaw; it shook or vibrated between the speeds of 60 to 80 mph.

I liked neither the shaking, nor did I like the fact that we had become hopelessly lost and it was getting dark. Maps were opened up and strewn about all over the car. There we were: three girls all with the girl-map mutation. When I saw the lights and heard the siren of the state police car, I felt relieved; I thought the officer might be helpful in directing us home.

Since I never had any experience with any of this, I slowed Ned down and simply stopped (in the left lane of a two-lane road). **"Pull over to the side of the road, you're going to get us all killed,"** his voice boomed over a loud speaker. He sounded mad. I noticed his face was really red as I was rolling down my window as fast as I could. "Don't you know anything?" I quickly responded: "I don't, I just started driving, and I don't even have my permanent license yet." I thought I'd invoke the *honesty is the best policy* doctrine.

I was pretty sure I could find my temporary license under a map somewhere. "Do you know you were going over ninety?" I responded by explaining Ned's shaking problem, the fact that we had been lost for so long, the problem with maps, how driving after dark with a temporary license was illegal, and how happy I was that he was there to help us home just like in the *Wizard of OZ*. After he completed his lecture, he escorted us a few miles to the road we next needed to take. I think he just wanted us out of his state. This would not be the last time when I was stopped by a fine civil servant and given a police escort to my intended destination (see *Blow Up*).

A couple of years later, while in college, I bought my very own car for six hundred dollars from a used car salesmen in one of those big lots with the eye-catching multi colored flags that just made you want to stop and buy a car. I found a cute green VW station wagon. Most of my questions concerned the radio and sound system. I was proud of myself when I asked the salesman if the car had any shaking problems. I really didn't know what to ask. And anyway, what was he going to say, "It's a two-ton piece of turd on four wheels?" I don't know who lies more: used car salesmen or women after sex, "it runs like a top," "no really, it was great."

About three weeks later, driving home from the beach with my high school boyfriend (we were still seeing each other from time to time), I said, "Do you smell smoke?" He did and encouraged me to quickly pull over. I thought I was doing the right thing when I pulled into a gas station and stopped the car by the pumps. Within seconds after we jumped out, the car was completely engulfed in flames. The gas station attendants were very upset, so were the firemen as they simultaneously rushed to evacuate the area and put out the fire. The cops, the firemen, the gas station attendants, and my on-again/off-again boyfriend were all yelling at me. I tried to explain how my mother always drove into gas stations when she needed directions or help, but this didn't seem to put out the *other* fire. We took the bus back to college in dead silence. As we drove back, I couldn't help but think how the fate of my car and the status of my relationship were somehow connected.

I was a tad cranky the next day when I *walked* back to the used car lot to confront the salesman. I figured I got my pound of flesh when I gave him another three hundred dollars and drove off with a *new* old car: a white Pinto. I hadn't heard anything about *The Pinto controversy* at the time, and anyway, it had a good radio. Soon after, I became very familiar with oil rings and valve seals, and in the process, made many new friends—all of whom had their names embroidered on their overalls. I began to refer to my Pinto as *bionic*. I was certain that the cost of my auto-education was low and that the resale value of my car would be high.

Whatever, I was in the middle of making my first film and needed a car to take a ton of film equipment around town to various locations. During that time, I racked up a few parking tickets . . . well, maybe more than a few. Parking wasn't always easy in many of the locations necessary for my film. In fact, I often had to choose between a possible ticket and having the car stolen. I was trying to be responsible. While having a lovely dinner on the east side of Manhattan one summer night, my bionic car was towed away and impounded until I was able to pay the back-fines from all those tickets. I was upset; it had been running like a champ.

Sadly, I didn't have the money to spring it from *car jail*. I called the great City of New York and told them that they had a fine vehicle on their hands and asked if they could possibly see fit to give me back my prized collection of *Life* and *Look* magazines I stored in the back of the car? The next thing I heard was a dial tone.

A year or so later while walking through Central Park, I saw my car being driven through the park. I was certain that it was my car because it still had my school decal on the back window and the silver gaffer's tape that was holding up the right side of the bumper. I started to run after it but lost it in a cloud of dust. I was happy to see that it was still on the road; someone had gotten a great car.

Have I run out of gas before? Um, yes. Have I had *post-it* notes placed on my dashboard that said, "**Pay Attention**"? Um, yes. Have I gotten my fair share of speeding tickets as well as parking tickets? Um, yes (A little advice: when an officer tells you the speed that you were traveling, **do not** use the word *allegedly* when responding to him). Have I forgotten where I've parked the car in huge parking structures? Um, yes.

While irritating and somewhat costly, all of the above have generally fallen into the *shit happens* category. Hitting things are harder to reasonably justify, but I will try:

I hit a garbage can, I swear it jumped out at me AND I thought I heard an anti-Semitic remark.

I hit a deep pothole, every other hole on that road, which was in the process of being repaired, had an orange cone by it.

I bottomed out our little sports car; it is engineered SO low to the ground. Ok, maybe I had a little too much to drink and was going way too fast when I hit that speed bump . . . maybe.

I backed into our gate, who left it open?

I had two other back-to-back car episodes that were less than amusing:

I was traveling down my street one night when an asshole in the oncoming lane veered dangerously close to me. I quickly moved right to avoid him and then BOOM, a large object that I later identified as a parked big brown UPS truck had clipped off my passenger side mirror; it might as well have been a camouflaged tank. I pulled my car over, the other car never stopped. The UPS man was so nice and wanted to make certain I was ok. To this day, I get a little squeamish whenever I see a UPS truck.

A few months later, I was in the parking lot of our local post office driving our little two-seater. I mention this to underscore that it was a really small car having no back-side whatsoever. I was taking my sweet time to park in an effort to avoid doing any further damage to the car or my marriage. I was almost completely parked when the blast of a car horn behind me hit me like a subway passing an inch from my ear. My foot reflexively pounded on what I thought was the brake—it was the other pedal.

The car lunged forward, hopping over that concrete parking block setting the front wheels between it and the curb. Exactly why are those concrete blocks there? My heart was pounding. I thought I was having a heart attack. The guy who honked looked like he was one hundred years old. He gave me the finger and drove off. Was there damage to the car? Um, yes. Did I have a witness who saw it all?

Thankfully, yes. Did my husband still want to kill me? Um, yes.

Why was I afflicted with such bad car karma? I went into deep contemplation of this affliction.

A year passed without any further incident until one early morning. With sleep, or lack of sleep, in my eyes, and the sun as an accomplice, I turned to make a *legal* U turn and mowed over a three foot tall STOP sign in the middle of the road that should never have been there in the first place. I completely flattened it. I had a lot of red on my silver car with a huge gaping dent that just screamed *expensive to fix*. The car was drivable and had a full tank of gas. I considered a run for the border. Instead, I pulled over, took a few pictures and called my husband to confess. He was eerily calm. I just left the car and walked home.

Hitting the *Stop* sign was the final sign. I thought about getting one of those black horse drawn buggies with the big orange triangles warning all to steer clear, or buying a Manhattan or British cab along with a driver. I considered several other solutions including my moving to Molokai, but I knew my kids would miss me. Between the back-end and front-end damage from this and another episode, it made more sense, dollar-wise, to trade the car in for a new one.

I was repentant and remorseful until we got to the dealership. I felt like I was in a bad *Lucy* episode: Ricky went off like a renegade missile that hadn't gotten the message to stand down. He began to angrily recount *every* driving and car related infraction I had ever had to a gaggle of sympathetic car salesmen on the showroom floor. Then it got personal: "Do you have an SUV with all-around idiot lights, imaging systems, and sonar? Obviously she only drives by sound." I tried to defend myself. It was pointless; the man tribe just huddled together with that look of: "How long have you been married to that crazy bitch?" By the time he asked for a *How Am I Driving* bumper sticker with his cell phone number on it, I was pissed.

Time passed. The man tribe went through the obligatory car haggle. Then it came time to pick out the actual car (SUV). For all of our relationship, and with the many cars we have bought together, my husband chose the car and I chose the color. I really didn't have much of an opinion about model or type, he didn't have much of an opinion about a color—with one exception: he hated white cars feeling that they looked *unfinishe*d. Guess what color, or lack of color, my new car happened to be?

My Car Karma has had a direct relationship to my relationships. I have found that men are very persnickety about things related to automobiles. Is it a boy/girl thing or just a *me* thing?

It is better for me to simply walk, and alone is probably best. Walking is better and safer, or, maybe not. My daughter was critical of my street crossing ability, or lack thereof as she saw it. She taught me how to properly cross the street paying careful attention to those little icons that light up at crosswalks. "Ok, mom pay attention—the little white man means it's ok for you to cross." Is it only me . . . does it bother anyone else that it's a little white man?

I did find my key that day at the beach. It was at the bench where I had stopped, or rather pulled over, to return a text.

Although I'm not a Luddite, I don't use the Fitbit any more. Don't get me wrong, I like it, I'm just more interested in putting one foot in front of another and taking it all in one step at a time.

Postscript:

I recently passed by the intersection with the stop sign that I had hit. Someone had mowed it over. It made me feel better . . . I was not alone in the universe.

FIRST LOVE

Who can forget the power and allure of a first love? Mine was exotic, having a beautiful smooth black body and Japanese ancestry. My first love was a Nikkormat with a fifty-millimeter lens.

I had always been aware of the beauty of light, how it varied and how it defined everything one could see. I liked the company of light and the comfort it brought. Or maybe, like so many others, I was just afraid of the boogieman in the dark; scared by what I could not see or know.

Anyway, I found that a camera was much more portable than a paint box and an easel, two items that had held some appeal. Mostly, I loved how a camera enabled adventures and opened my eyes to so much.

So, back to my love:

I could not wait to spend time and be alone with my Nik. The day after I brought it home, I decided we needed to solidify our relationship by taking a trip to the East Village and Lower East Side of NYC. This *field trip* meant that I would not be able to attend school that day. Since tenth grade had just started, I didn't think that I would really have missed much, and I knew I had plenty of time to catch up on whatever I missed.

It was a brisk high-contrast fall day. I took a few shots and was walking down a small somewhat desolate street when, from my left side, I felt someone suddenly push me into a doorway of what looked like an industrial or abandoned building. I vividly recall his dark brown eyes and his dirty green parka. His hands were on my new love, which was strapped across my chest, "Give it to me." I never took my eyes off of his when I said, "You'll have to kill me." My heart moved up to my throat but I was not moving off my position nor diverting my eyes from his. He sighed deeply and in disgust ran off.

Love is crazy. It brings you to your emotional and rational edge.

Even after this little episode, I again soon found myself gently rocking on a Metro North train with my baby, bound for NYC on yet another fine school day. Like every other day in Manhattan, millions of people packed the streets. I strolled down Lexington Ave on the other side of town where I knew my mother would be extremely involved with her workday . . . or so I thought. What were the odds? There she was. We passed each other, and both took a beat until we turned around in utter shock and disbelief. She said two words to me, "Go home," and so I did.

Love.

As time went on, I became less obsessed. I let my love affair settle down, and slowly, very slowly it and I matured . . . probably a good thing. I figured we'd have our whole lives together . . . and it has been a fine and enduring relationship.

IT'S A MATTER
OF DEGREES

I really liked and respected the doctor who delivered my kids. Both pregnancies were high risk by virtue of my age, and the fact that my mother ate fistfuls of DES throughout her pregnancy. Toward the middle of each pregnancy, I went to see him to have an ultrasound taken almost every other day. We became fast friends. He had multiple degrees, an MD, JD, and an MBA. How could he be so insensitive and thoughtless? This must have been very difficult for his mother, "My son the . . . ?" My doctor just loved learning and achievement; above all he loved delivering babies. I had total faith in my decision to put my twisted cervix and unborn children in his hands.

On one of my office visits while waiting for my daily *jelly on the belly*, I began to count all of his diplomas and certificates of accreditation, which I affectionately referred to as *placemats* . . . eighty-six, eighty-seven, eighty-eight. I was running out of fingers and toes three times over, when in he walked reading my chart. "Do you know your blood type?" He didn't even give me a chance to respond, "A+ . . . figures." I started to laugh, "Well, Mr. Smarty Pants, if you must know, the last actual diploma *Miss Know It All* got was from junior high school." Now I really had his attention. I went on to explain, "I did graduate from college having completed the requisite coursework, but High School was another story. And, I did have sort of a hostage issue with my College diploma." Now, with a high degree of smug curiosity, and seemingly all the time in the world he then said, "Tell me more."

I had a funny relationship with school. I viewed it as secondary or complementary to my learning, and at times, optional. I didn't get off to a great start. It took a few years for the grown-ups to decide that I wasn't stupid. By grade four it was discovered that I was dyslexic and likely had some other faulty wiring.

My kindergarten to third grade teachers dealt with me by speaking slowly or very loudly, or by putting me in solitary confinement in the hallway outside of my classroom (that was big back then). At times they thought I was disruptive for asking questions like, "How small can small get?" Luckily for me, a teacher did take me seriously and offered to tutor me afterschool. With her help, I learned how to read toward the end of third grade. I also received answers to my many questions from a family friend who was a physicist and worked in a big science lab in Brookhaven, NY.

Generally, I thought that school made students the way Ford made cars. I had much more of a customized view of what and how to learn, and once I began reading, everything was grist for the mill.

I glided through elementary school. Mostly I remember: dodge ball, lunch, softball and the friends I made there. Two people, who I will never forget, were the teacher who taught me how to read and the school janitor who recruited her help for me. We used to talk while I helped him clean up after lunch. I guess he didn't think I belonged in the garbage pail.

I went on to a big junior high school that was a tad unruly. Large gang fights broke out on a regular basis. I have a few significant memories of those days:

- A science teacher who taught us how to tell when a boy really likes you (pupil dilations and contractions).
- A Spanish teacher who was having an affair with the French teacher and often gave us free study periods during class time so he could be with her. He'd come into our class and with his very thick accent he'd say, "Ok class, do your 'omwork and study your herbs (I did once take out a library book on herbs: growing and cooking with them, fascinating)."
- An Art teacher who made me aware of Saint Exupery, the beauty of Maine and other general nifty observations about life.
- After years of having taken those *fill in the dots* standardized tests, I was sick of them. Who wasn't? When in eighth grade faced with yet another, I turned my test

paper horizontally and drew a fine farm scene utilizing as many of those dots as I possibly could. Eventually the test came back with "VOID" stamped all over it. For years, it proudly hung framed in my guidance counselor's office; I liked her.

- I read *Invisible Man* by Ralph Ellison. I understood how people could occupy space but not be seen.

High School was a very big improvement. The adults seemed to have more control over the environment. I had many fun memories from high school:

- I was sitting outside of English class waiting for the bell to ring while reading the Bible. This was not an assignment. I just wanted to see what all the fuss was about. I was very absorbed in Genesis, so much so that I did not hear the bell ring or see the movement of students around me. I was not in any way trying to be a wise-ass when my teacher came out to yell at me, I simply got lost in all the "begets." "But I'm reading the Bible," my explanation seemed to manifest a response of biblical proportions; he made the Pharaoh look calm.

- I put a lollypop wrapper in the waste paper basket belonging to the Vice Principals' secretary. I liked the VP. We met on several occasions and had many interesting conversations. The secretary started to yell at me for not having asked her *permission* to use her waste paper basket. Really? I must have missed the rule about garbage disposal. She looked like a pink puffer fish when the VP emerged from his office to investigate the ruckus. "Get into my office right now," commanded my friend, and when he closed the door we both burst out laughing. I think he went on to become the school Principal. I thought that was a fine decision.

Somehow I passed through all of my coursework and requirements in order to graduate, well almost. One needed to pass a swim test and take a typing class. I was never a strong swimmer, but ability was not the issue here. Our school pool was disgusting: swamps had more appeal. I made every excuse not to go in it from having my period for three consecutive months to having *contagious dermatitis*, a condition that I simply made up. As for the typing, my mother was insistent that I acquire this skill as a prelude to a *good job*. Enough said.

I did see some value in high school. There were several teachers I really liked; most especially an art teacher who I took classes from as often I could. Even with my love and respect for this teacher, my struggle with consistency and convention remained. It did not help my GPA when, in twelfth grade, that same art teacher asked, "What grade shall I give you" (I had decided to do other things when I *should have* been her class)? I flippantly answered by saying "I've never gotten a *1* (out of one hundred)." She was very happy to fulfill my fantasy.

Meanwhile, the notion of college loomed. I had a vague

idea of where I wanted to go, never mind that I didn't have the grades to get in, that detail didn't concern me. All of that changed when a friend slowed her car down as I was walking home one day and said, "Want to take a drive upstate to visit my cousin and look at her school tomorrow?" By my quick calculations, the school she mentioned put me in close range to my high school boyfriend who was attending college.

We had a great time that weekend and after spending an hour or so with someone in the college admissions office, I checked the box for early decision and had my application finished in less than two weeks. A few weeks after I sent them a love letter, I received one back. Their envelope was much bigger and included a generous scholarship and a financial aid package, so by late November, the mystery of college was solved. They wanted to see my first semester grades, and they never asked for anything else.

I found that I loved college and the people there. But after two years I had a stronger idea of what I wanted to do in life and ended up transferring to another school. Again, at my new school, I had many positive experiences and great teachers. In addition, I was able to fit my course work around many out of school interests and projects: most notably an independent documentary I was doing off campus a few states away.

Eventually, I completed all of my requirements and felt pretty good despite the slight hangover the day I took my place at our commencement ceremony. I walked up to get my diploma and inside the folder instead of a *placemat* with a bunch of Latin and my name, there was a note from the Bursars office informing me that I owed them $912. If I ever wanted to see my diploma, I needed to pay up.

I went to the office the following day with a spring in my step, fifty bucks and a few marbles in my pocket intending to work out some sort of amortization plan to pay off my debt; even with the marbles, no dice. You're kidding, right? I had put myself though college with a mix of financial aid, scholarships, student loans, and jobs. I politely thanked them and thought, "Keep your fucking diploma." My annoyance quickly subsided and I soon forgot all about it.

For a split second, post-college, I did consider grad school (MBA), but I thought my intention was poorly motivated. I wanted to go through the program and then find some reason not to get a diploma, so that I could lay claim to being the best educated junior high school graduate walking the face of the earth; I was relieved when that moment passed. I was trying to exhibit some maturity.

Years later, and after a successful career beyond my imagination, two children with a man who, like my OB/GYN, has many *placemats*, I still had only my 5X7 junior high school diploma to fix on my academic wall of distinction.

My college diploma was eventually sprung from debtors' prison thirty-two years later for the $912 I owed by my husband, who had run out of ideas of what to get me for my birthday. He also did not want our firstborn to get away with taunting me with her recently acquired High School diploma.

Looking back, would I have done things differently? Yes. As I sit here pecking away on my keyboard at 2 miles per hour, I wish I had learned how to type, and I wish I hadn't been so glib with my high school art teacher. Conversely, I am glad to know that I can learn almost anything, and while not everything is brain surgery, I am smart enough to know how to get out of the way when one is required.

And . . . yes, I probably would have had more of an edge in life if I had less of one. It is all a matter of degrees.

SERENDIPITY & FROZEN HOT CHOCOLATE

I love the yummy wonderland that is Serendipity, (the restaurant in New York City known for its signature frozen hot chocolate) as much as I love the idea of serendipity.

For a variety of reasons, I decided that it might be a good idea to take some time before transferring to my new university. Several of my friends from college were taking terms abroad in various locations across Europe. Naturally, I wanted to visit them. I also entertained this vague notion of wanting to interview European filmmakers whose work I studied. How would I get there, and more to the point, how would I justify taking time off from school to be there? I needed a plan.

During high school I had been a busy little bee building a photo business with my boyfriend. We took pictures of kids at various day camps all across New York and sold our wares to their parents for $5.50 per package. Our costs were $1.25 plus the X percentage in kickbacks to the greedy camp directors. Even still, the money we made was considered a small fortune by any measure; the only kids doing better than us were the ones selling drugs. Most of my share of the profits went toward paying for college, but there was some money left. So, while I had the funds to travel through Europe, I didn't exactly have the enthusiastic support of my mother, who felt I had an unrealistic view of *work in the real world* and that *bumming around* Europe trying to get the attention of some famous filmmaker was a fool's errand. Let's just say I had a different view of the world.

One day while doing *real world* work: cleaning up our apartment and collecting the newspapers to toss down our building incinerator, I saw a headline that caught my attention. The United Nations declared 1979 *The International Year of the Child* and planned various activities around the world to celebrate it. I thought the UN was such a kid-friendly place: they had all those colorful flags and they let you take your shoes off and bang them on tables. Cool.

I wondered: would they need a photographer for this 1979 initiative? Before long I was sitting in an office at the UN with my camera and an arm full of pictures taken of kids from my camp photography business. "Wouldn't it be good to have a kid (I was twenty, but whatever) take pictures of other kids for your upcoming celebration of us? I happen to be planning a trip to Europe anyway and, by the way, I used to love collecting money for you with those little orange boxes during Halloween."

The UN representative thought that was a *smashing idea* and she too was a big fan of Halloween (I loved the Brits). She gave me an itinerary, a contact list, a letter of introduction, and a mission to travel to several countries to photograph. If the pictures were any good, they would use them in various publications and in a planned traveling exhibit. As soon as my meeting there was over I made a *beeline* to Serendipity for some frozen hot chocolate, it was a very sweet day.

I had my stamp of *travel legitimacy* and I was able to use my newly acquired diplomatic skills, from having spent a day at the UN, on my mother. Over time, she grew more comfortable with all of my plans.

To help fill my dance card while in Europe, I made a few contacts so that I might be able to interview some of my European film heroes. If possible, I would publish these interviews in film magazines. Some of the magazine editors I spoke with practically dared me to connect with the people on my wish list; jeez, adults really have a hard time taking kids seriously—maybe the UN's efforts will change all that. The cherry on top of all these plans came when my best friend from high school decided that she would travel on this great adventure with me. Sweet.

All in all, it was an incredible few months with many great experiences photographing for the UN, doing a few interviews of famous filmmakers, playing with my friends, meeting new friends, and having many great adventures (adventures you will read about in upcoming stories—I'm trying hard to stay focused on how serendipity factored into my life).

A few weeks after my long trip, I dropped off a package of negatives and prints to the very nice British lady at the United Nations. When I left her office it started to rain. Not wanting to get my portfolio case wet, I ran to catch the bus as it closed its doors. The driver was merciful and opened the door allowing me to take the one seat left on the bus.

I was cold, soggy, and a bit cranky when the woman seated next to me decided to start a conversation. She seemed undaunted by my indifference; obviously she must have been from out of town. Before long, I was chattering away about my trip and, of course, she asked to see the pictures in my portfolio case. Reluctantly, I opened it up and showed her the few prints I had left. Then she asked if I had ever heard of *Vista*. My blank stare must have tipped her off; "How about The Peace Corps?" Bingo, I wasn't that dumb. She handed me her card (she was the Communications Director of Vista) and said that if I'd be interested in photographing for her, she'd be happy to meet—very, very sweet. That chance bus ride would later bring me into a world that would forever change the direction of my life.

My assignment for Vista was to shoot in various locations where their people worked. The first place on the list was in the South Bronx where a community group and Vista volunteers were working to rebuild the neighborhood. It wasn't long before I knew that I had stumbled into a very special place with an extraordinary group of people.

It took a little doing, but I convinced the Communications Director that it was better to concentrate my efforts in one place. She agreed, and, after a couple of months there, I successfully completed my assignment. Then, I thought it would be a good idea to go back to school before somebody closely related to me got really, really mad—and so I did. However, I had a very strong feeling that my work there wasn't finished.

At school, as I sat in a Film Studies class, I decided to do a documentary film on that very special place and group of pioneers in the South Bronx. I was certain that my school would be supportive. After all, the area attracted Presidents and other politicians (Charlotte Street), and it was only a hop, skip, and jump away from a famous fort (Apache). My next thought: how does one go about making a film, does the money fall from the sky courtesy of the documentary film gods? Maybe the Indians around the fort would know? I know, I'll ask one of my teachers at school: "This is not a technical or trade school and you have taken a considerable amount of time off." I was on my own. I went to the library and started to study, not structuralism or semiotics, but how to make and fund a documentary film.

My first grant proposal was to the National Endowment for the Humanities. I never thought I would get it; imagine my surprise when I did. It took three years, and a lot of on-the-job learning to finish the film. Making the film was the most challenging and rewarding thing I have ever done in my little career, and eventually, I even graduated from college, which pleased my mother to no end.

After college, I moved to NYC and went to work as an Associate Producer for a small television production company. It wasn't long before I began to do business development (finding work) for them. To that end, I had a meeting set with someone at a very big advertising agency to pitch a television show for one of the agency's clients. I immediately hit it off with the person I met with: our conversation effortlessly moved from one topic to the next until he said, "So, lets talk about the job?" Job? I paused for a beat and then said, "Tell me about it." As he spoke, I silently prayed that whoever was supposed to show up for this job interview would not, at least while I was there; I didn't want to be tossed onto Madison Ave by a big hulking security guard. I sat there and listened as my new friend described this really cool job that fate and I had decided was mine. And, days later, it was. Super, super, super sweet.

My first day working for this really big ad agency was at a NATPE (National Association of Television Program Executives) convention. There I was with all the *movers and shakers* in the TV biz; they were doing all the moving and I was doing all the shaking. A guy came up to me, noticed my nametag, and immediately started to tell me about a huge deal he had discussed with my boss. When he realized I was an idiot, he left.

I was at the agency for six amazing years before moving

on to a new chapter of my life in Hollywood where *make believe* and the unexpected seemed like an ordinary and expected part of my everyday life—and for so much it, it was.

All in all, very sweet . . . like frozen hot chocolate.

BLOW UP

(Note: This is one of the few times where I will name drop with reckless abandon.)

Youth is a funny time. One is often clueless about many things, especially about *what's right* and *what's not* and thankfully so. I'm not advocating wholesale stupidity here; I'm suggesting that this is the perfect time in life for a certain amount of risk taking and exploration.

Early on in life, I had been exposed to all sorts of interesting thinkers, writers, filmmakers, artists, and such (such were often my favorite group)—just lucky, I guess. During my first couple of years at college, I studied the work of various European filmmakers. I thought I'd like to meet some and ask them some insightful questions, and naturally I thought that they would want to meet me. I was sure, if I asked nicely, that some of these filmmakers would be amenable: some were, some not so much. Generally speaking, the French filmmakers were not as eager or welcoming as the Italians filmmakers. *C'est la vie, connards.* I made several inquiries to my Italian film heroes and, instead of being given the boot I was directed to it.

So happy was I, when I was invited to meet and lunch with Franco Salinas: one of the writers of the screenplay for *The Battle of Algiers*. I was very prepared for this interview, which was to take place at his seaside apartment just outside of Rome. I also hoped that he would help connect me to the film's director and co-author of the screenplay, Gillo Pontecorvo. This story has less to do with how my interview went, and has everything to do with how I went, literally.

I had very detailed instructions to get to my appointment using public transportation. I had been in Europe for a few months and in Italy for many weeks. Despite the fact that I didn't speak the language, I thought of myself as an expert with the buses and trains there. The morning of my rendezvous (I'll extend an olive branch to my French friends by using one of my favorite French words), I leapt out of bed, showered, had a quick breakfast, checked my camera equipment, and made sure I had my little list of dumb-ass questions, which at the time I thought were brilliant.

I got to the bus station early only to find that the public transportation workers were on strike. WHAT? Fucking revolutionaries! Didn't they realize that this was my day of destiny to meet a revolutionary whose film was so controversial when it came out it was banned in many countries (including France—just saying)? I should have thought more about this. In Italy, strikes were as common as *canti* bars but not as fun.

Ok, when in Rome . . . *Plan B* was to just simply rent a

car. Since I could only order food and curse in Italian, I went back to enlist the help of the lovely proprietor at the *pensione* where I was staying: she was so helpful, problem solved. Soon thereafter, I signed my life away on a bunch of documents placed before me. Then the car rental gentlemen directed me to my chariot . . . cute little car, nice color, does it have a radio? What's that stick coming out of the floor? What, a stick shift? Nowhere in *Plan B* did it say anything about learning how to drive a stick shift in the middle of Rome. "No, no, no, I need-a automatic-a transmission!" His look transcended every language: "This is Europe you dumb bitch, take it or leave it." Like I said, youth . . . I took the car. Thus began one of my most noble and memorable experiments while on my travel adventure, and definitely one of the top while in Italy.

I stalled out every two seconds, people screamed, horns blared, and all sorts of hand gestures flew as I concentrated on trying to just keep the car on the road. It wasn't long before I looked like I had taken a dip in the Trevi Fountain. Not only was driving the car a big issue, but I also had no real idea where I was going. All those signs in Italian looked and seemed the same to me. And what's with those traffic circles with the confusing red arrows every 2.3 seconds? I went around some of those circles multiple times like a blind and drunk racecar driver at Le Mans (at this point I missed France). I was so happy to have made it outside of Rome without hurting anyone or creating any more *ruins* tears streamed down my face.

When I stalled out for the eightieth time, I got out of the car just to kick it and to try and get my bearings. In the distance I saw some birds that looked like ones you'd see at the beach. Like every great explorer, I decided to follow them. Since I was in my own pool of sweat, I began to play Marco Polo to distract myself from my introduction to abject fear. I reached what looked like a beach community. I kept driving and followed the birds. Finally, I saw a sign I recognized; it felt like a religious experience. I vowed that if I made it out of this alive for sure I was going to light a candle or two for Saint Somebody at any and every church I came across for as long as I was in Rome, so help me G-d; please. I saw a parking spot near where what I prayed was my destination. It required parallel parking. What, what, what did I ever do (rhetorical)? I must have attempted to park the car twenty times or more before a guy came over and parked the car for me. It was Franco Salinas.

I swear on St. Somebody and on the head of my kids and my unborn grandbabies, that this is a true story, sadly. I just wanted to die and yet I was so grateful that I hadn't. I tried to explain the trials and travails I encountered to get to him. After a couple of minutes, I just really didn't care. All I wanted was the tall glass of wine that his girlfriend/wife poured for me. It took a while for my hands to stop trembling. They were both very nice. I don't really recall much of our conversation—I was totally preoccupied by thoughts about my return trip.

We ate lunch, I took a few pictures, and somehow I managed to ask some reasonably intelligent questions, enough so that he gave me the contact information for Pontecorvo, who was in Madrid prepping a movie. He also pulled my car out for me—bless him. I had decided that, once I got the car moving, I would not stop, no matter what. I just wanted to get back to my little *pensione.*

For my return trip, imagine more of the same only this time having had a drink or two and driving in late afternoon traffic—**in Rome**. I was practically hanging out of the window trying to warn all others to steer clear when a siren from a police car caught my attention and me. This was the second time in my young life to have the police stop me and to be grateful that they did. I was pulled over by not just any old police officer or traffic cop, but The National Police, the *Carabinieri.*

There were three officers in the car, and two came over to welcome/rescue/arrest me. I tried as best I could to tell them the story; neither spoke English. Out of the corner of my twitching eye, I noticed the officer in the police car was laughing his ass off and soon approached his two friends and me. A lot of Italian was spoken followed by laughter. Nervously, I laughed too. The English-speaking officer told me to get into *the passenger* seat and then, with an advance car with its siren blaring, he proceeded to drive my car back to the rental car place where it belonged. My Italian rescuer was very nice. I just kept apologizing and saying how much

I loved hazelnut gelato and being in his beautiful country. When I got back to my little room, I fell onto my bed and didn't move until the following morning. The next day I walked all over Rome, and each time I saw a church I went in and lit a candle.

Several days later, I scheduled my next interview in Rome. After this *Blow Up* I was very grateful for a driver to the apartment of my next appointment, this time with Michelangelo Antonioni. I am a lucky girl. I was nervous and for a variety of reasons but relieved to find that this experience with Antonioni had none of the excitement and life or death gravitas of my previous experience.

Aside from being an exceptionally talented filmmaker, Antonioni was an elegant and handsome man. We had tea and/or coffee, and I cannot remember if food was involved. I don't think I totally embarrassed myself. The one thing I vividly recall was how I got home. When it came time to leave, he picked up the phone and made a call. He then walked me to the door of his apartment to a big staircase. Down from it stepped Monica Vitti, his one time leading lady in life as well as the leading lady in many of his films. I followed her to a car that was waiting to take her somewhere in Rome. She smiled as we drove in silence. I was very appreciative of the ride and happy to have been *The Passenger*. It would have only been better had it been Jack sitting beside me.

I eventually left Rome and was making my way to Madrid to meet Pontecorvo. Fate intervened, and I never made it there. Instead I had a worthy adventure, which likely these filmmakers would have appreciated, one that held much more value than having asked a brilliant filmmaker a few dumbass questions.

Fin

THE LITTLE NEIGHBORHOOD THAT COULD

The South Bronx was quite an active and talked about neighborhood during the 1970s. It kept the New York City Fire Department very busy. As the neighborhood deteriorated and property values and rents went down, flames went up. Landlords made more money from insurance companies than from rent rolls. The area looked like a set for a war or a disaster movie with plenty of *extras* to play shell-shocked refugees with nowhere to go and nothing to lose.

The South Bronx also attracted many politicians who declared it a national tragedy, made lots of promises, and then left. It was not a good time for a place that once provided homes to, and childhood memories for, many people: Murray Perahia, Al Pacino, Colin Powell, Sonia Sotomayor, and so many more. But things were not as Black, White, and Hispanic as all believed. Among the cops, firemen, pimps, drug lords, arsonists, hookers, and thieves were many hard working people who called the place home and, who shockingly had the same hopes and dreams for themselves and their families as almost everyone else living in Elsewhere, Earth.

While doing a photo assignment in the South Bronx, I met many people with great vision and courage. In an act of civil disobedience, a group of neighborhood residents came together and literally stood in front of a bulldozer, ordered by the city of New York, to demolish an apartment building in the middle of their block. Simply, they had other ideas for that building. Rather than destroy it, they wanted to rebuild it with their own sweat and labor. They formed a community group to raise public and private money in order to help accomplish their goal. In the years that followed that infamous day, this organization, Banana Kelly Community Improvement Association, saved that building. In addition, it repaired hundreds of units of other neighborhood housing, built parks, planted gardens, provided employment, and trained scores of young people for a variety of different trades and management positions in the years that followed.

I thought they were truly amazing. They were pioneers on the frontier of what most people saw as hell—they viewed it differently. Before long I found myself making my own promises to the residents there: "Someone should make a film about you guys." Since many people there had never before put up drywall, I felt my lack of experience in film-making somehow made me uniquely qualified for the job. "I'll do it . . . I'll make this film." I thought I was just like them, and while I wasn't certain of how to make this film, I was certain of why it needed to be made.

I left and, a few months later, came back with my first grant. It was for fifteen thousand dollars. Wow, I thought to myself, I could do two films for that amount of money—I was so stupid. Fortunately, I returned with two other people without whose involvement I would never have been able to fulfill my promise. My crew included a fellow film student from my university and an equally talented cinematographer my brother knew from his school. They were a salvation especially during the early days when I'd pick up the film camera and say, "How do you turn this on again?" Thus began a stop and start production that spanned over a three year period and took multiples of the original grant amount to complete.

We started to film close to the beginning when picks, shovels, and hammers were being put to work by the early pioneers there. In a show of solidarity, (plus it looked like fun) we joined in, working construction alongside everyone else. It was pretty quickly determined that I was not the go-to person for measuring things. I did get a few splinters and put some nails where they didn't belong, but *overalls* I did ok.

A big part of my job was getting the resources to produce the film. I channeled my very best Willie Sutton and went where the money was. The next couple of grants came from the charitable arms of two big banks; they weren't huge hugs, but I felt the love and appreciated it. At that time in the late 70s, the large banks were in warm to hot water with various federal agencies for *redlining* (underserving) poor communities. This was thirty or so years before they figured out how to market, bundle, and package loans to poor and working class people, and to make tons of money from the practice. This meant that community groups in poor neighborhoods, and people shedding light on them (me), were the recipients of their largess. The bank people I met were extremely intelligent, thoughtful, and supportive. In fact, I dated one for a short period of time.

The next grant was from another group of filmmakers: Time Life Films. They were in pre-production on a film, *Fort Apache, The Bronx*. The film script was highly controversial making many local residents uncomfortable with the way in which they were being portrayed; think savages. The media was all over it, and protests and pressure mounted.

I thought the film company *might* find it valuable to support another film being made in the area, which had a wholly different point of view. I reasoned that their support of our film would give the film's PR department something to use to counter all that negative publicity (I try to be helpful). Luckily for me, they saw it the same way. Two lovely ladies, who were very known publicists in the film world, represented Time Life Films in my dealings with them.

They decided to give us a five thousand dollar grant, but it took forever to process while our film footage remained unprocessed. Meanwhile, little stories of our love affair began to emerge in the NYC press. In an attempt to expedite the payment I stepped into my office (a phone booth) to encourage them along. It was a hilarious call, not with what was directly said between us, but because they *thought* they put me on hold when having a sidebar conversation about our deal—jeez, they curse like I do and they think like I do. I thought, maybe I could do what they do. A few days later we had our check, I forgot about the call and the possibility of working in PR, but the experience reinforced what my instincts already told me about how to play *the game*.

The stop and start of production was beginning to wear on my brake lining and patience. I began to imagine my future grandbabies wondering aloud about when Grandma would finish her film. It was at this point that I knew I needed a bigger and better plan. I decided that the same strategy that worked for the local news *might* work for the national news. So I wrote another letter, "Dear Mr. President," as in Carter.

President Carter had kicked a few cans around Charlotte Street in a surprise visit to the neighborhood in 1977. Several years later, his political rival, Ronald Regan, was quick to point to the lack of progress since Carter's historic trip. In fact, Reagan's indictment was not true. Progress was being made, however slowly and quietly. I am not a historian, but one could make an argument that President

Carter's stroll through the land of *once was* provided the necessary impetus for the land of *now is*.

At any rate, I thought political hay and sway during the election year might provide the necessary funds to finish the film. To my surprise and delight, the letter was answered, and shortly thereafter we were put in touch with the Deputy Secretary of The Department of Health and Human Services who decided that he should come to visit us. This was a big opportunity for both the community group and the film.

My partner at this big pow-wow was the Executive Director of the community group. In the thirty-five years that have passed since first meeting this person, I have yet to meet anyone with the combination and quality of attributes—vision, intelligence, leadership, and courage evident, and in abundance, in this person. He was a friend and was an invaluable supporter in the making of my film. And you know that saying: "Behind every great man . . ." this expression was very applicable here (and still is).

We had a great meeting with the HHS official that concluded with the screening of excerpts from the film. Several weeks later we received word that our grant request of thirty five thousand dollars to complete the film was approved. Shortly thereafter, President Carter lost the election and President-elect Reagan froze all approved government grants including ours.

It wasn't long after Johnny Carson and Frank Sinatra finished Reagan's Inaugural show, that I started writing yet another letter: "Dear Mr. President," as in Reagan. Several weeks after it was sent I received a reply with new contact information for new people in the administration to help defrost our funding. At this point, I was beginning to wonder if one could make a living by writing to presidents. Like with the PR ladies, soon after we received our money to finally complete the film I forgot about that possibility and simply got back to work.

We finally finished and broadcast the film on WNET in New York, where it won a local Emmy award. As promised, the film was given to the community group. It was an incredible experience; only a small gesture in comparison to what the *little neighborhood that could* did. I was just happy to be along for the ride.

WARE?

I was not a believer in *time travel* until I experienced it. The matriarch and patriarch of the family prominently featured in our documentary invited me to a family reunion at their family farm in Ware, Mississippi. Even though it was a big detour for our film, I thought it might be valuable, and I was always up for a road trip. Together with my boyfriend and the co-director of the film, we packed up our gear and headed south.

We crossed from the heart of Dixie into the Bayou State with the slow twang of *gee-tar pickin* on the radio. No matter what speed we traveled, the heat and humidity of mid-August slowed the car to a crawl as it trespassed through dense white space; it was if we were driving through a marshmallow that was being slow roasted on an open fire. We were very hot and sticky.

And speaking of white, we had several experiences that made us feel as if we had been transported back to a time where using the word *Negro* would have seemed as quaint as saying, "person of the Jewish faith" in 1930s Germany. It was 1980 and in the Deep South using the words *nigger* and *kike* were as common as porch rocking chairs, so we found.

And speaking of crackers in rocking chairs, when we rolled into town, a kindly looking old gent rocking on his porch greeted us warmly **until** we asked for directions to the farm owned by the nice black family who was hosting us. He clammed up mighty quick after we mentioned we were filmmakers (aka: trouble making, black loving, commie Jews . . .), and uttered a few choice words as he got up and went inside his house probably to get his white sheet and shotgun. We left. The next person we asked for directions was a person of color across the invisible tracks that were very real to the folks down there in Ware.

We were relieved to make it to our host's farm and their family reunion. They treated us like royalty and gave me the only room with air conditioning. I shared it with Grandma. This family was warm, gracious, and the picture of self-sufficiency. Everything they needed they grew or made themselves with two exceptions, butter and milk, both of which they purchased at great cost at the local grocer in town. Even though there was a pasteurizing facility only a few miles away, milk was three times more expensive in the stores where *colored people* were welcome to shop. Somehow this did not surprise me. I told them that I hate milk but loved the grits they made for breakfast. While there, I was also introduced to catfish and okra.

On Sunday morning we were invited to services at our host's one room church. We asked if we could film parts of the service. When we put up a few interior lights, the inside temp rose to two hundred degrees, or at least that's what it felt like. It might have been hot as hell, but the music was heavenly. We grabbed some footage, turned off our lights, put down the camera, and joined in feverishly fanning ourselves with handheld fans adorned with pictures of Martin Luther King and John F Kennedy on them.

Afterward, to cool down, our friends suggested that we go to the *white side* of the lake for a swim. White side? I only knew about *black sides and white sides* as in cookies. We were strongly encouraged to follow local customs, so we did.

It didn't take long before I found myself playing with a couple of cute kids at the water's edge. It felt good to be in that cool water. The kid's parents wandered over and we began to chat. I told them that we were just passing through the area enjoying the good weather and fine southern hospitality. I knew to keep my mouth shut in regards to any subject outside of pleasantries, so we talked about a lot of general things as we tossed their kids into the water. Then, I asked why milk was so expensive. They seemed surprised and asked where I had been shopping; and explained that it was only really expensive in the Black grocery stores.

To this day, I still don't like milk but always order grits whenever I see them on a menu. I felt bad for those kids I met at the lake that day. They were so cute and sweet. I wondered how they would grow up, and if they would ever be allowed to have a black and white cookie or be able to make a s'more.

We didn't use one frame from Ware in our final cut. Even

though it was the same family, it was two different films in two different worlds and times. I was glad to have taken the trip but was happier when we returned. Maybe, in time, we'll figure out how everything fits together.

BRAND LOYALTY

When I first began my job at the ad agency, I quickly took note of the fact that very few people had any idea, or real interest in, what my boss and I did. The objective was to start a programming department and to generally think about *the big idea*. My other stellar observation was that *brand loyalty* must be very important because people spend a ton of energy and money to get it.

The person who ran the media department, who was always talking about *the big idea* (*Mr. Big Idea*), was a very smart and forward thinking guy, and did I mention patient? It took us, my boss and I, some time to develop a strategy and convince our clients to join in on all the fun. A big part of our plan involved resurrecting the sponsorship of television programs (think GE Theatre). It was very forward looking of us to look backward. We did generate some fresh ideas to make this a new and value added proposition for our clients. After almost a year of dragging our presentation around, we signed our first big client.

The first guy in turned out to be one of the most innovative. His company had a multi-million dollar media fund dedicated to high-risk experimental ventures out of which, over time, we managed to take a big *chunk-y* (think soup). He (*Mr. First Guy In*) was a warm and wonderful person with a wicked sense of humor. He became one of my most beloved mentors. I was very lucky in my professional life: I collected mentors the way Liz Taylor collected husbands.

At my first presentation to *Mr. First Guy In*, I gave a detailed analysis of a deal we recommended. With his eyes peering above his signature half-glasses perched at the tip of his nose he said, "Look, any idiot can give me a best case scenario, tell me about the worst case and how you plan to avoid it." I never again wasted anyone's time presenting a *best-case* scenario. After getting *Mr. First Guy In* and his company on board, it was much easier to convince other clients to put their butts on the line. Duh.

My boss and I became the *go-to* people for all things Hollywood. We spent a lot of time on planes flying to LA, meeting with network and studio executives, independent producers, writers, bartenders, waiters, and others with a story to tell. Some early observations about LA: it was odd to drive up to a restaurant and just give your car to some guy (this did not work (then) back in NY), everyone was late to meetings, or mostly we were, (traffic) and LA had some very nice hotels.

The first hotel I ever stayed at in LA was the Hotel Bel-Air. I felt like Alice stepping into Wonderland each time there. The agency had a long-standing deal with the hotel, and I was one of the lucky beneficiaries.

By the time I passed my first anniversary with the agency,

I came up on my second opportunity to attend the Emmy Awards. At the last minute, a client and I decided to go. I asked my secretary (that was the correct term back then) to book me at the Hotel Bel-Air. When I arrived, they seemed especially nice and escorted me to a room close to the pool. It was much bigger than usual with a neat fireplace and a living room. Sweet. This was going to be such a wonderful week, where's that room service menu?

The Emmy's were memorable too, especially the after party. I had just finished saying, "hi" to someone I finally recognized, when I turned to leave and literally bumped into this mass of black and white. It was a tux belonging to someone with shoulders in two different time zones. I looked up to see Tom Selleck smiling down at me. I almost passed out. FYI, I was never star-struck or celebrity-disabled (except for this time). I recovered. It was a fun night within a terrific week.

When I went to go check out at the end of this terrific week, I thought I was really going to pass out. My bill was eye popping: "There must be some mistake." No mistakes were made on their end, only mine. The amount I owed was more than twice the GNP of many island nations. It was a very long plane ride as I contemplated how I was going to pay the agency back, and what my future without a job would look like.

My boss suggested I take my little issue up with a more senior guy within the department before word got out, and the company's stock crashed. Later that day, I gathered my courage and walked into the senior guy's office. He closed the door and started laughing; my emotions went in the opposite direction. "Here's what we're doing to do, pay the bill and we'll expense this as separate trips over time and, by the way, try not to do this again." I loved this guy and so many others there.

Shortly after the *Bel-Air Affair* (mine was with a calculator), someone at another ad agency approached me about a job opportunity. The person who approached me was very well respected in the industry and had obviously never heard anything about my expense account mishap. I told my boss, and he suggested that I go and talk to him. Was he trying to get rid of me?

My conversation at this other agency went well, and before I knew what was happening I was marched upstairs to meet with his boss. We spoke for quite some time until he stopped me and said, "Look you have this job if you want it, but I have to say, you seem very happy where you are. Happy should not be underrated. Sleep on it and call me tomorrow." Then, as he ushered me out the door, he mentioned what the job paid. It was more than double what I earned—boy this guy was smooth.

By the time I crossed town on my way to my little apartment, I had already made up my mind. I was going to take his sage advice and stay where I was happy. I called him the next day to thank him; I think he was truly surprised. Later that day he called *Mr. Big Idea*, his counterpart, and told him the story. Shortly afterward, *Mr. Big Idea* called me into his office, thanked me for staying, and as he walked me to the door said, "By the way, we're increasing your salary by ten grand." Very smooth, did these guys go to the same finishing school?

Over time, my boss and I developed a thriving little business within the agency eventually working on almost all of its accounts. We worked with various producers and hatched all sorts of schemes to benefit our clients. This gave us great access and opportunities.

I was lucky to get on the radar of a *legend* in the ad business. It just so happened that he was the creative head of our agency. This came about because of a deal/project I generated that ultimately never materialized. It involved a woman who was at the beginning of a very successful daytime talk show and who was also a talented actress having just finished her first feature film. We'll refer to her as *Ms. Talk Show Goddess*, just for fun. I wanted her to do a couple of TV movies for my favorite client, *Mr. First-Guy-In*.

One thing led to another, and before long we were talking about having her do commercials for the company's flagship brand. The *creative* (commercials) that our *shop* (ad agency—don't you just love buzz words) came up with were, in a word, brilliant. Everyone loved how this was unfolding . . . well almost everyone. In order for this to happen, our client would have to take their flagship brand away from another agency and give it to us; a decision that involved tens of millions of dollars.

Although this did enter my mind, it was not the primary

motivation for suggesting this project. I thought it would be a really good thing for *Mr. First Guy In* and his company. All of the business deals and *creative* quickly fell into place. It was time for *Ms. Talk Show Goddess* to meet the President and the CEO of the company. We made sure we pulled out all the stops by sending a company plane to Chicago (you've figured this out by now, right?).

It was her first ride on a small private plane and her lawyer wanted to be certain that she would be safe. I made a couple of calls. I found out there was a guy in charge of planes (corporate transportation) and he assured me that it was not a crop duster from the Dust Bowl era. Just to be sure, I called my brother who flew many small planes, "Is a Gulfstream a safe plane?" It was a very good flight and a very good meeting.

We moved this project ever closer to reality until the guys who ran the other agency, who had the flagship brand, were dialed into the conversation. Funny, they were not as enthusiastic as we were. I never got all the details, *Mr. First-Guy-In* was a very classy guy, but from other sources I heard a lot of groveling was involved. Maybe it had something to do with loyalty or lawyers and large sums of money. I'm not sure. At any rate, the deal came off the table. *Ms. Talk Show Goddess* never did a corporate product endorsement. I'm sure she was asked by just about everyone on the planet.

This episode put me into another orbit at the agency, and I had many other great experiences and opportunities there because of it. I never thought seriously about leaving until one *Godfather* day when I was made an offer that I couldn't refuse. I was headed to Hollywood for a new job there. I had many difficult conversations with people I loved and respected and who gave me so much within the agency and among our clients.

My most difficult conversation I saved for last: it was with *Mr. First Guy In*. I called and told him I needed to talk, and when I walked into his office and no words came out. I just stood there. Then I placed my new employment contact in front of him; he always appreciated a good deal. With his signature glasses on the tip of his nose and his eyes looking into mine he responded with perfect comedic timing, "Well, looks like your going from Soup . . . to Nuts," and then he started to laugh. I burst out crying.

By the time I left the agency, I pretty much knew my job. I also knew a bit about brand loyalty . . . it's priceless.

ABSOLUTELY!

Instead of the more traditional reply and demure delivery to "Do you take this man to be . . ." "Absolutely!" is what I shouted out to the few hundred people assembled for our wedding. It took several minutes for the room to quiet down. The Cantor struggled to keep her composure for the rest of the ceremony; I enjoyed hearing the prayers she sang amid her unintentional pauses and chuckles. I didn't mean to be a wiseass; I just needed to break the tension. Up until this blessed event my mother and father hadn't laid eyes on each other for twenty-five years.

I met my husband a few months before we both graduated from the same university. After six years of post-graduate boyfriend and girlfriend status, many of our friends and family were tapping their toes waiting for it to change. Not wanting anyone to get restless leg syndrome, we decided to break a glass.

I hailed from a couple of generations of dysfunction and divorce (as close as I'll ever get to a double D) and he was from the *Walton's of Massachusetts*. My father and stepmother offered us a generous amount of money to either quietly start our lives together or to use for a wedding.

While I loved a good party, I was from the camp of *take the money and run*. My soon-to-be husband was more inclined toward the three-ring circus—I mean party.

In some Jewish weddings men and women are seated and observe the ceremony separately. In ours, we had *my mothers camp*, *my fathers camp,* and in between . . . the demilitarized zone. To be fair, this was not an issue with my father or stepmother. As for my mother, well lets just say she had a chip on her shoulder and leave it at that.

I don't know what we were smoking when we decided to put a year between our announcement and our wedding day since this gave my mother 365 days to torture me.

Nonetheless, the show would go on with me as the producer. The music topped my priority list followed by catering and wardrobe. The first two items on the agenda were a piece of cake, but I wasn't certain about that *top of the wedding cake* look. Every dress I liked seemed a bit disco and was very expensive; I had no idea people paid that kind of money for so little of a dress. Of course I wasn't exactly shopping at Wedding Dresses for Less, I was in the Wedding Department of Bergdorf Goodman's. I was chatting up a sales person laughing as we went from *traditional, timeless, and tasteful* to *isn't she a slut*. I did not want to give my mother more reason to be pissed, nor did I want to get off on the wrong foot with my mother-in-law, so I leaned toward the three T's.

Most of the dresses I liked were budget busting. As I looked in the mirror, I thought I saw a dress laughingly stare back at me while saying, "What are you kidding? You can't afford me." Then my new friend (the sales lady) asked, "Are you superstitious?" "Well, you notice I'm not wearing a strand of garlic, why?" She went on to explain she had a client who bought a very expensive dress and had had it altered three times while she lost weight, when husband-to-be backed out weeks before the wedding. She thought the dress would fit me like a glove, and she could sell it to me for the price of the alterations, which was about ten percent of what the dress cost. Ninety percent of me could deal with this. It was a bit spooky how well the dress fit. I looked great. I wrote her a check and invited her to the wedding.

The only other person I was responsible for dressing was my twin. I only needed his suit size and an hour of his time for him to decide which of the pre-selected suits he wanted. This dynamic was very much in our playbook, and I must say, he looked great that day too. Everything seamlessly came together and the party was fun to plan. As time grew near, so too, did the tension with one so dear, my mommy.

The morning of our wedding, I woke up determined to have a good time. I got to the temple, changed from my sneakers, jeans, and T-shirt into my dress and began to take some pictures with the wedding photographer's camera. Eventually, I gave it back to her.

The next stop was the Rabbi's study to sign the Ketubah, a Jewish marriage contact. I had never seen one before and asked for some time to read the fine print. This generated a little laughter for all in the room, which included my husband's best friend who was there to sign as the witness to the whole Ketubah thing. Instead of signing on the *witness* line, he almost signed on the line where I was expected to sign. We laughed our asses off as we wondered aloud about how to announce the new couple.

It was now time for the showdown. Since I didn't want that droopy alcoholic look in any of the wedding pictures, I swore I wouldn't have a sip of anything. I was a bit edgy when I entered the reception area where our immediate family waited to be seated before the wedding. I noticed my mother who looked like she was about to be administered the Last Rights. Distant relatives miraculously revived her until my father and stepmother entered the room. I needed to do something, so I took my mother's hand and walked her over to my father and said, "I believe you two know each other." They exchanged the requisite congratulatory remarks; no punches were thrown. Then I walked her away, hand in hand, and delivered her to welcoming friends and family. That wasn't too bad, mission accomplished . . . or so I thought.

By the time the *perp walk* down the aisle commenced, nothing could conceal my mother's discomfort. Just a note here, my mother was happy that I was getting married and loved my future husband—everyone did, even my brother, who disliked and dismissed all of my former boyfriends (those I introduced him to). This was not how I wanted to get this party started so when it came to the *I do's* I gave it my best: "ABSOLUTELY!"

The response was an audience pleaser and relief; it set the

tone for the rest of the event. The music was great, the food was good, the drinks were flowing, and the room began to mix and flow.

The after-party was at The Carlyle Hotel and involved good friends and many bottles of Champagne. The next night we were on a plane headed for Rome. When we landed, a tank met the plane on the runway. I turned to my husband (it was so weird to use that term for the first time) and said, "Look a wedding gift from Mom."

When we returned, it took about a year before my mother would talk to me again. Years later, I told this story in much more detail to a writer who thought it would make a terrific television movie which we set up at ABC. It was a fun script to develop (some parts did feel like therapy) and the only project in the history of me where I did *absolutely* nothing to push the script toward production once it was finished. What was I thinking?

Looking back, and despite all the issues, would I have done it all over again? ABSOLUTELY.

ONE FLEW OVER
THE CO-OP BOARD

Buying real estate is very adult. I avoided it. But then it happened. It was the late eighties and post-marriage when, lo and behold, we had an accepted offer for a one-bedroom apartment in the high eighties on West End Avenue in NYC. It was a beautiful pre-war building. The apartment was advertised as "needing tender loving care," read: dump. No problem, I had spent lots of time learning all sorts of handy trade skills during my documentary days with the homesteaders in the South Bronx. My husband wasn't as convinced but agreed that we could do some things ourselves.

The only thing left to do was the co-op board interview. I didn't mind this step but hoped that there would be no way for them to discover my post-college parties, the ones where New York's Finest often stopped by to say, "hello." My husband was much less sanguine about having to jump through this hoop. They had all of our financial statements; we could well afford the apartment. I thought of it as a formality and suggested that he should be Zen about it, big baby.

When the day of reckoning came, and we faced three board members and answered their many questions I became, well, like a junkyard dog. I had more than a noticeable edge and insisted upon asking them a few pointed questions as well. "Perhaps it would be good to take a little break," my husband wisely suggested after the first twenty minutes or so. We stepped into the hall. "Are you crazy? If you want this apartment you better shut the hell up and calm yourself down." I thought that was a reasonable suggestion, and when we went back into the apartment; I hit all my marks and gave an award-winning performance. The female co-op board member was unmoved and kept giving me nasty looks, but happily majority ruled. Welcome to home ownership.

The renovation work commenced. My husband was very busy at work, so I hired many of the people we needed to help us lovingly restore our apartment to its pre-war glory. I gave them lots of cash upfront before they started work, and fortunately, most of them returned. *Live and learn* became a familiar refrain.

Our painter thought we should *skim coat* the walls and ceiling. I like smooth walls, and so we went for the added expense. I burned with curiosity to know what freshly skim-coated walls looked like, so right after work, I ran over to the apartment. It was a thing of beauty. He had done a fine job. While there, I noticed that it was chilly for some reason. Ah ha, some idiot had turned off the radiator. I turned it back on and quickly felt nice and toasty. Then I closed up the apartment and went home for a relaxing dinner.

The next day, my phone was screaming off the hook. It wasn't the only screaming I heard; I thought our painter was going to have a heart attack. He informed me that all, and I mean all, of the plaster melted during the night from the radiator heat and steam that somehow managed to escape. I ran to the apartment; it looked like *Jabba the Hut* had melted, what a mess.

Had one of the other workers left the heat on? Did the Super enter the apartment? The painter and my husband were busy spinning theories. I tried to lighten the mood by suggesting we look to the bitch on the co-op board as a possible suspect. No laughter on the second floor. I did not want anyone to take the blame and later that night confessed to a really, really pissed off husband. As he yelled at me, I reminded him of the time he tried to replace a toilet seat cover in our old apartment. He couldn't loosen one of the lug nuts and used a hammer to try. Moral of that story, never use a hammer on a porcelain toilet. Ok, let's let bygones be bygones. I found myself using many insipid platitudes during this home renovation process. I promised to stay out of the apartment and everyone's way and before long the work was completed. Next came the cosmetic part; this was definitely in my zone. I was back in the game.

Everything was going, dare I say, smoothly. We went

shopping for gray Berber carpet at a very big store: ABC Carpet. While they had tons of rolls of grey Berber carpet on the floor, the specific carpet I wanted, the one with the tiny fleck of cream color running through the weave, was on back order. I was willing to wait for it. I felt strongly that the cream highlight made all the difference in the world.

We paid for the carpet and set up an appointment for someone to come to our apartment and measure (no one seemed willing to go with my measurements). I had to take the day off from work to wait for the person to come measure. He was a no-show. I had to take another day off and this time he came and measured.

Weeks after they said the carpet would arrive, I had to take yet another day off for it to be delivered and installed. Finally, when they rolled it out, it was two feet short. Ok, shit happens . . . at least it wasn't my fault. We went down to the store the next day and selected new carpet; this time, a grey Berber that was immediately available. It was a hundred dollars more than the original, and we were given the bill for the difference. Are they kidding?

The man who was helping us really couldn't care less about my story and directed us to the cashier. After all that, no way was I going to give them a penny more. Then I heard "Suit yourself," from the salesman further adding to my anger and frustration. Talking to the manager was not any more effective, and he just walked away to help another customer. At that point, it was as if somebody said *Niagara Falls* . . . I just lost it and shouted at the top of my lungs,

"This place sucks, it's a rip off—don't shop here!"

Everything stopped. Everyone froze. All of the salesmen scurried into a shaking huddle. My husband looked at me as if the next stop on our pleasant afternoon together would be Bellevue.

The carpet we selected was delivered and installed the very next day without any additional cost. As I sat there waiting for it, I did some research on the topic of anger management.

We lived happily in our apartment for about a year before fate intervened and we moved to LA. Not knowing if we would stay past the two-year commitment I had made, we decided to sublet the apartment. I found a lovely young couple, both bankers. Banks always seemed so clean and shiny. I felt that this couple was perfect; they would be responsible and would maintain our apartment as if it were their own, no need to convene a co-op board.

Two years passed. We loved LA and decided to stay. We also got a letter from the Nazi bitch at the co-op board letting us know that according to their rules we could no longer rent our apartment. My first thought was to convert our apartment into a homeless shelter. After I calmed down, we decided to just sell the apartment. The NYC real estate market had crashed. We were hoping to sell the apartment without having to write the bank a check.

When our renters left, I discovered that our apartment was far from clean and shiny. They were pigs: how not surprising. We hired a cleaning crew, and I decided to give the apartment a fresh coat of paint before putting it on the market. I was planning to buy my mother a new car and thought I'd get both done on my next trip to NY.

I drove into the city with the new car I had just bought on a beautiful spring morning perfect for a day of mindless work painting. Oh look, there's a space right in front of the building. I am so lucky. I parked and went around the corner to get my day's paint supply. On my way back I was whistling a happy tune as I walked down the street, when I noticed that all the cars parked on my block were gone, including my mother's day-old car.

I ran to find the doorman, doormen know everything, and learned that it was street cleaning day after nine . . . just like the sign said. My car had been towed. Damn, damn, damn. My doorman knew exactly where the car would be and wrote down the address with the warning that I had better show up with a banker's check or cash when I went to go spring the car. Did he have to mention bankers?

I called my husband and woke him up in LA. I always forget about that time-change thing. He knew I was upset and handled it well until I became frustrated with him over not knowing the location of the nearest ATM machine or how I was to use one. To explain, my husband does the banking, and I had not been in a bank in years since a bank representative kindly asked me to take my business elsewhere. I found an ATM machine, and with a little help, got the money. I did notice how clean and shiny the bank was, damn bankers. Then I called my mother to let her know that I'd now be late for dinner. When I told her what had transpired, she let out such a blood-curdling scream that to this day it still gives me shivers when I think about it (think Janet Leigh in *Psycho*).

Soon after I talked my mother down from the ledge, I was in a cab heading to the Westside dock area to get the car somewhere on Tenth Ave. The cab driver dropped me off at the wrong place: my dock was several blocks away. I started to walk. Every other car honked and slowed down as I walked along Tenth Ave. What the hell? What do these guys want? When I looked around at all of the other people who walked near me I realized they were scantily clothed women: Prostitutes! Really? Do I look like a fucking hooker in my sneakers, painter's pants, and white Haines T-shirt?

Finally, I got to the car and handed the guy there a bazillion dollars. He handed me the keys and the parking ticket. I didn't care. I was just so relieved to get in the car. I drove it directly to our old parking garage a few blocks away from our old apartment. The guy there remembered me. He was very nice, "How's LA?" to which I responded, "You'd like it there, it has a lot of cars." Then I handed him the key and a twenty-dollar bill, "Please, take care of this car." Hours later, it was time to go paint.

I was so happy when I completed my work. The apartment looked good. Maybe we shouldn't sell it? Nah, I had enough of home ownership. I closed the door and as I exited the lobby, I bumped into the Nazi bitch from the co-op board (who was probably married to a banker). "How nice to see you, how is everything?" she asked. "Really, really well, thank you." And then I said goodbye to the doorman and walked away.

TOUCHED WITH
SINGULARITY

The expression above originates from a legendary television executive and producer. When he first said this to me, I let it float by as I tried to determine its exact meaning. Was this space-time singularity; was he talking about Artificial Intelligence and the end of mankind by technology run amuck?

In our few meetings together, he had always gone out of his way to mention his educational pedigree, Harvard, and how the Ivy I attended was a poor stepchild. Whatever. Having said that, I didn't want to give him any additional support for his thesis. I needed to know what he meant by that expression. So I asked him, "Um, about that expression . . ." He quickly cut me off and told me to figure it out myself. Did I really need this? This was in the day of *Dewey Decimal* long before Larry and Sergey. Couldn't he have just told me? I spent far too much time researching this phrase, in general and in the context of our conversations, which with him were usually a string of stories and random non-sequiturs.

Months later we met again for breakfast at The Polo Lounge, a place that for him was touched with familiarity. We met to discuss a potential project for client sponsorship. I came to breakfast with my homework on *singularity* and with the hope that I might unlock its meaning and score some points with Harvard-boy. We ordered breakfast and before long bits of stories and random thoughts rocketed through the Polo Longue like a ball expertly hit by a king. Notice, I didn't say queen; I did my best to keep pace. Then, all of a sudden, he got this look on his face and said, "I have to go . . . I just thought of a great idea for a movie, I have to go sell it." He got up and just left before I got a chance to discuss that expression.

It was exasperating. I sat there and ate my breakfast; his was untouched. A young agent I knew came by and sat down to join me. I asked him if he wanted the uneaten toast abandoned by my breakfast date. As I sat there and watched my young friend spread jam across the toast, I decided that *Touched with Singularity*, meant people who were *characters*: colorful characters—one of a kind, larger than life originals like this producer who coined the phrase. Someone could come and take a bite of his breakfast; but no one could eat his lunch. Luckily for me, I have met more than a few people *Touched with Singularity*.

One person who immediately comes to mind was the first outside counsel we hired at the ad agency. As we made some pretty big deals with folks in Hollywood, we wanted to be certain that we'd leave the negotiating table with all our fingers and toes so that our heads wouldn't later be handed to us.

To that effect, we met an entertainment attorney with over thirty years experience who soon became our guy. He was tough, charming, and elegant. Did I mention he was tough? This was the first time I ever saw someone who habitually weaponized intelligence and who viewed every call or conversation as a battlefield. Deals that could have taken a little bit of time took a lot, and they were always contentious.

The flipside: he could be extremely charming and had great stories about his life in Hollywood particularly about famous actresses whom he dated. Writing and penmanship were paramount with this guy and he used only the best pens. I learned quite a bit from him. Words that echo: "Always say it like you mean it." I did notice that he said *like* you mean it not *because*. I figured it was one of those clever loopholes of which lawyers are so fond. Sadly, I had to make the decision a couple of years later to replace him. I said it like I meant it, but it was hard. We parted as friends and he gave me a gift that I cherished: a beautiful wine-colored Mont Blanc pen.

Another person *Touched with Singularity* was someone with whom I did my first television movie. He had an incredible career and produced dozens of movies that won multiple awards. I happened to see a news story about a high school football coach who brought his team to a state championship while confined to a wheelchair because he suffered from Lou Gehrig's disease. It was a moving piece perfect for a CBS Sunday Night Movie, or so I thought, as did about twenty other producers who also wanted the story rights. I called this producer, and we decided to go after it together. I jumped on a plane and met his wife who produced and directed many of the films his company made. It took several trips and several weeks to finally win the rights to make the movie. Both he and his wife were masterful in every aspect of how they worked through this process. The movie turned out well and went on to win its time slot—always a welcome outcome in TV-Land.

For many years, regardless of if we had anything in production or development together, this producer was the first person I would call each morning when I got to work. Fortunately, he was always up involved with another of his passions, horse racing. We'd go over deals (mine) to make sure that I did not overlook anything, or talk about writers, directors, other producers, naughty and nice network executives, ideas for movies-anything and everything. When in LA, he'd often take me to the horse races. I learned a bit about that too: let him place the bets.

We did only one other movie together. The film was a very important project that mattered deeply to his wife. It was on a tough subject: child molestation. Every network had passed on it. I turned to the client who I knew would see its importance and have the guts to help make the movie possible. A year or so later the movie was broadcast on

ABC. Everyone did a great job to sensitively bring a very tough topic into millions of living rooms. I am making this sound as if producing television is easy, its not. The odds were always long to get anything over the finish line, but not with these people. Both he and his wife were a sure bet, both truly touched with singularity.

When I left the agency and went to Hollywood, I went to work at an animation company. Naturally, I thought I was well qualified for it since I liked cartoons and doodled a lot while in school. We had a unique mission. The company was soon to have a *For Sale* sign up. We had a few years to make some noise to create a more dynamic environment for its sale.

Within eighteen months the company sold to someone who could be the poster child for *Touched with Singularity*. The new owner planned a visit to *kick the tires* of his new possession. My brother had worked for this person in the early days of another of this man's ventures, affectionately referred to as *Chicken Noodle News*, CNN.

This guy, my brother, and several others took a little trip to Cuba to interview its president for this *fledging* network. A picture of this small group was taken late one night after a few drinks were had. My brother gave me a copy of the picture and I brought it in with me the day of the new owner's visit. When he walked into my office, I showed him the picture. "Where did you get this?" he seemed genuinely taken aback. I pointed to my brother and said, "Mi hermano." He paused and then with perfect timing said, "My life has come full circle . . . first I work with the brother, now the sister." No doubt why this guy was touched with singularity.

I was in the middle of production on a television movie when the animation company was sold. Long story, but the movie ownership transferred to another production company. The new owner of the film wanted my continued involvement with the film, something about not changing horses midstream. I was delighted; it gave me the additional benefit of working with yet another legendary producer who was one of the most celebrated and successful in the history of television. He had a very big house.

We were in the edit room one day, after the editor's rough-cut, to work through the film for the first time. He (this producer) was masterful in the editing room. We reached a point in the film that gave us a bit of a headache. I offered a suggestion for a cure. It was as if I had just detonated a bomb: the editor looked like he anticipated a fall-out.

The producer said nothing to me and instructed the editor to make the cut that I had suggested. It worked well and we continued forward. I pretty much kept silent after that. My last meeting with this producer was in his office. It was a huge office filled with tropical fish tanks. His desk and office were as clean and sparkly as the tanks.

I took a few notes of last minute things we needed to do, said good-bye, and went to get my car. As I got into my car I realized that I had left my pen upstairs on his desk. It was the wine-colored Mont Blanc pen. No problem, I called his secretary to let her know that I had to come back upstairs to retrieve it. I knocked on his door and entered to see him where I had left him, sitting behind his desk. "Just came back for my pen," I announced. "Don't see it, no pen here." I looked at his desk and then at him. "I know I just left it here." He just shook his head "No, not here . . ." Maybe one of the barracudas had swallowed it.

Legendary . . . he was . . . *Touched with Singularity*.

ROCKIN'
THE CASBAH

My father and stepmother took my brother and me on a family trip to Morocco during a summer break from college. This was our first big trip traveling with them and other members of our family. We were very excited.

My twin was ALWAYS late each morning and barely managed to get his ass on the bus before the tour left without him. Our aunt would always defend him and would bring him breakfast as he stumbled on board the bus each morning.

From one city to the next we found ourselves in the middle of a medina trying to make certain we weren't kidnapped (Midnight Express had just been released) or taken for a ride. While the former could have been possible, no chance of the latter as our Aunt raised the art of *haggling* to a new level. It was more exciting than a sporting event.

My brother had a habit of wandering off seemingly lost in the maze and haze of the markets. On one of our last days there, my little nomad was, as per usual, late, when all including the bus driver, threatened to leave without him. I got a bit panicky when, from a distance, I spotted him among the teaming masses that spilled out of the market. It wasn't hard to recognize him: at six feet three inches he stood out like a minaret. With a deep tan and curly brown hair, he looked like a Middle-Eastern giant complete with a big smile, a Fez, and *magic* carpet in hand that he proudly showcased to all as he boarded the bus. He was a little snake charmer, that boy.

By the time we lived in CA, my twin had circled the globe more times than Neil Armstrong. He had collected friends from all over whom he liked to mash up at huge parties he threw each summer. Every time he came to visit us in LA, our phone rang non-stop, and I was his social secretary.

After a while it began to bother me that he spent so much of his time while in LA traveling from one friend to another. I wanted more time with him. I had a great idea: we had just bought a house with a good indoor/outdoor party flow, "Why don't we have a little shindig here and invite your friends?" I thought that was a perfect solution: I'd get to plan a party with him and we'd be able to spend lots of quality time together. I had so much fun planning the menu and watching him as he made his legendary music mixes.

I began to wonder, as the phone rang for the hundredth time, how many friends could he possibly have here, 30 to 40? To this day, I've never seen so many people in our house and I've had some pretty big parties here. It was quite the rave filled with all kinds: from a group of German stewardesses he had just met, to television personalities, comedians, a politician, and even a tree house architect. Old and new friends mixed as easily as the cocktails, and in the middle of it all, drink in one hand cigar in the other, was my twin, a boy seemingly born under a star who held court in a maze of humanity, all, *Rockin' the Casbah*.

THE STUFF LEFT ON THE EDIT ROOM FLOOR

Television is a funny business. Politics, timing, programming considerations, and maybe a few decks of tarot cards, determine what gets produced and what does not. A studio executive, who once interviewed me for a possible job, took out her Ouija board to see if we'd be a good fit. I could have answered that question shortly after we met. As I entered her office, she hopped around on a pogo stick and continued to do so during the first few minutes of our meeting. It was a challenge to keep eye contact. I let about fifteen minutes or so pass until it *felt right* for me and then excused myself because I *remembered* that I had left my car running. I was very happy to get back to my old job.

During my days at the ad agency, I developed over a half-dozen made-for-television movies, and, when I left to run the TV department of a once mighty animation company, I saw no reason to stop.

A good friend at William Morris wanted to introduce me to one of his clients, Joanne Woodward. She planned to produce and star in a television movie that she and her husband had developed as a feature at a major film studio. Joanne and William Morris wished to place the script with a production company to redevelop it for television. My friend set up meetings for her to meet six or so television producers; all of who, were multi-award winning producers in the prime of their careers. I was not. I was under thirty and worked for *Yogi* and *Boo-Boo*. In other words, I basically didn't have a chance in hell, but I was grateful to be considered—plus, any excuse to travel to NY was always welcome.

I went to meet her at a restaurant near her apartment on the Upper East Side of Manhattan. I was a tiny bit late, damn traffic. Joanne sat and patiently waited as I approached her. I swore I saw a halo around her head; she smiled and just radiated *other worldliness*. While I can't recall all of the specifics of our lunchtime conversation, I remember well her Southern charm that made our meeting easy, comfortable, and warm. I also vividly recall her skin; it was like looking at a fine porcelain doll. Urban legend was that she took milk baths: I began to reconsider my position on milk.

We talked generally about how best to tell the film's story and how to prioritize the elements within it. The story centered on the first wrongful death lawsuit against a tobacco company. A husband and wife legal team brought the suit to court during a time when their marriage was falling apart. The key was to find the right dramatic balance in the story. I had no real idea if anything I said hit a responsive chord. She listened and was very polite.

I stopped my ramble and then, as an aside, mentioned that she and her husband had been long-time customers of my father and stepmother's housewares store on Madison Ave. She smiled and warmly acknowledged the reference. I got the check, paid, walked out of the restaurant, and expected never again to see her. Her next comment forever cemented her star on my Walk of Fame, "Let's go to your dad's store, I think I need a few things." When we walked in together, the look on my father's face was priceless. I *reintroduced* her to him, and she proceeded to complement him on having a fine daughter. Since my father seemed to not always understand what I actually did for a living, this was very reassuring. She left empty handed, and I had a father filled with pride.

A few days later when I was back in LA, my friend from William Morris called: "she picked you." I let out such a big "Yabba dabba doo," Fred would have been impressed. Thus began one of my most rewarding and yet frustrating experiences in TV development (hell).

The first part was easy; we set the movie up at ABC and negotiated one of the richest production deals for a TV movie ever made. All we needed was a script that Joanne and the network would *green light* (agree upon). Next, I sent her a short list of writers I thought perfect for the adaptation.

She had her own list: a few NY based playwrights, some without any TV credits, all excellent writers. After several months and many meetings, we finally selected a talented husband-and-wife writing team who we felt would bring added dimension to the work.

During our months long search for the perfect writer, CBS approached Joanne with another movie project that she found compelling. It also required a rewrite to meet her approval. Our deal with ABC was predicated on the production and broadcast of our film in time for November sweeps, a critical time for the networks. We also needed to be first and only movie with her starring. All of a sudden we were in a race to the moon with the Russians (CBS).

We must have done six drafts before she was ready for liftoff on our project. During this period, I decided it was time to aggressively push: we began the search for potential directors and co-stars. I also asked our legal department to vet the script for Errors & Omissions (E&O) insurance, an important and usually routine step . . . but not this time. It seemed that the former producers of this project were less than tidy about obtaining the rights of those actually involved in this story. She was very upset to learn about this. This oversight was more than just a little wrinkle that took time and much diplomacy to fix, and shortly afterward, we finally had a script that Joanne was ready to make. Now all we needed was script approval by the head of TV movies at ABC . . . he had *notes* (changes). This was as welcome as poison ivy at a summer's picnic.

I set up the call to discuss his concerns. It was all very cordial, and when it was over, I knew Joanne would not want to make the suggested changes, but she was a gracious professional, and we did do a revision. ABC was thrilled with the next draft. She was not. Days later she decided to move ahead with the CBS movie. It was crushing. Many months later I met her for tea in her apartment in NY. She made brownies.

I have had more than a few scripts that I've loved implode for one reason or another. While this is the nature of the beast, it doesn't mean I have to like that big hairy monster. A couple of these scripts came from the same writer. One was early in his career written with his former writing partner. The other script was years later when he wrote on his own. Both pushed the boundaries of taste—in fact, they were re-markably offensive. I loved these projects as much as I hated the spineless network executives who all passed on them. Oops, did I say that out loud? That writer went on to create *Desperate Housewives* just as I became one.

A favorite project that never got past the pilot stage was a contemporary Western for CBS set in a fictional Colorado town where strange and supernatural occurrences were as common as flies on a horse's ass . . . and speaking of horse's asses, there were more than a few involved in this project. One of the writers on this project was as difficult as he was talented. He had an acute allergy to network and studio executives, but somehow I did not make him itchy. He and his writing partner, his then wife, were simultaneously writing two pilot scripts for me at two different networks (CBS & ABC).

The odds of both projects getting a pilot order were about as high as me turning into a petite blond, and then they both were picked up for pilots (think Reese Witherspoon: she would have been fourteen then, but whatever). Since the ABC project was extremely expensive, they asked that we produce the pilot as a two-hour movie. Ordinarily, I would be happy about this, but in this case I had one team of writer/producers on two productions with one requiring a new and much longer script for the two-hour movie while we simultaneously produced both pilots. It was insane. Just to make this time in life even more relaxing and pleasurable, two other projects out of our small company were given the green light, one with a full season production order. At this point I thought of myself as a pig/horse hybrid, with an emphasis on its ass, to have had agreed to all of this, particularly the two-hour pilot.

Two series: one, a sit-com, the other a series of Reality specials went forward. The two-hour movie pilot was produced and broadcast. It was conceptually strong, but that was about it. Even though it did respectfully in the ratings, it was a project I wish I had never known.

And now for my favorite pilot that never made it to a series: it had a legendary director along with a great song written and performed by the show's star. One of the hottest music guys in the business produced the song. I even had a promo made by one of the best feature film marketers since I hated the promos the network made. This show was *the perfect package*, yet, we were **not** given a series order.

It's always been a good thing that I valued the process as much as the product, sometimes even more.

As for as many projects that hit the Editing room floor, there were also many others that did broadcast, and I am grateful to have been a part of them all. My one regret: I wish I had been able to stay away from the peanut M&M's during editing. The excess *chub* from that time is like residuals, which continue to resist diet and many types of exercise. Maybe a pogo stick is in the cards?

THE UPSIDE-DOWN
MOM CAKE

A s a kid I used to make Betty Crocker's Easy Pineapple Upside Down Cake in my Easy Bake Oven. It was easy and fun; nothing like when a kid has to take over when a parent's life turns upside down.

You don't know when the moment will come but when that moment arrives, you'll know it. For me, that time came after a long plane ride on a surprise visit to see my mother. As soon as she opened the door of our childhood apartment, where she lived alone for twenty-two years since my brother and I had left, I knew that moment had arrived. Life was now upside down, my mother needed a mother, and I was in charge.

Among other things, our mother was fiercely independent, elegant, stylish, and prideful, bordering on vain, and from *that generation* where it was completely impossible to go anywhere without being *just so*. She had recently turned eighty and had taken a new picture to renew her driver's license—she looked twenty years younger. But in that moment, in clothes that were dirty, without her *face on* and with a slight odor from not having apparently bathed in quite sometime, she looked like she had aged those twenty years in the two months that had passed since I had last seen her. She was disoriented and barely functional.

The next morning I brought her to her doctor's office to make certain she was well enough to travel. I had been in phone contact with her primary care doctor and an ENT (Ear, Nose, and Throat doctor) because of her sudden loss of hearing. Suffice it to say, I was not terribly impressed with what I heard. I sensed that my mother's abrupt turn was not a garden-variety illness, and that it would take more time and expertise to figure it out.

I packed her bag and we headed to the airport where I bought two one-way tickets back to LA.

The first couple of weeks into my mother's *visit* at our house were exhausting and filled with doctor appointments: hers and my own. I was many months pregnant. In between all of this, I tried to keep the TV production company I ran from flat lining and my four year old from being bored (thank you Sponge Bob). On one particular night, I came home and did what was usual when I was completely exhausted and without answers: I put my head down on our kitchen table and closed my eyes. In walked my husband to offer some support and perspective, "Why so glum? Just because you're forty, pregnant and living with your mother . . ."

My mother was *true to form* in her illness as she was throughout her life. Her illness was difficult to diagnose and remained a mystery until a couple of weeks before she passed away. This puzzle meant many, many, many visits to multiple doctors, all of whom had the same paperwork to fill out with slight variances depending on their area of specialty.

This seemed crazy to me, there had to be a better way. Did they only use technology for billing? My favorite revelation from my dip into the Healthcare cesspool was that no offices communicated with each other. I had to carve out a ton of time to pass important information between the small army of doctors who were now on the frontlines of her care.

Another observation from this time and my experience: if you are old and sick, dye your hair. Old people are triaged, and, as such, people tend to move like old people when they treat old people. To those who acted in this way, one expression comes to mind: *what goes around comes around*. This ageism awareness was an eye opener, and it made me think about my own generation. The baby boomers are not going to go gently down this road. If nothing else, there will be good protest songs written.

Our mother always lied about her age; this too seemed to be generational. Example: when we met with a new doctor. He sat behind his desk across from my mother. I stood behind her. "So, Mrs. *X*, you're how old?" "Let's see, (she paused to think about it, long enough for me to think, "it's a fucking number, just give it to him") I think I'm seventy-five," she responded as she tried to determine if this was a good number for her. I gestured madly with my arms . . . higher, higher. It was such a ridiculous scene. I much later discovered that she also lied about her age to Social Security and in doing so lost two years of her benefits.

Taking over my mother's finances was also hardly a piece of cake. She claimed not to recall where her bank accounts were. I really did not need or welcome this little shell game; forensic accountants would have been stymied. It turns out she had money spread out in over a dozen banks all over the tri-state area. As a child of the depression, she was afraid of bank failures. I was afraid of brain damage for all of the machinations required to organize her life. When it was all finally accounted for, she had more money than we imagined; much of which we used to provide excellent care for her later in her own apartment.

Closing her apartment in NY was a challenge and took quite a bit of time to bake, but it did produce some laughs. A few months after daughter #2 was born, I found myself back in our childhood hellhole with one of my best friends. We began the daunting task of burrowing through a life-time of stuff. My mother had given me a list of *must haves* for her new apartment. A few hours later, my twin finally showed up with a big smile and a miner's helmet on; it was so him.

Rummaging through her things was bittersweet. Our

mother had been a buyer for Bloomingdales in the late 1940s and early fifties. During this time she traveled extensively and had a collection of one of a kind hats from when she bought millinery. She always assumed that one day she would donate this collection to the costume department of the Metropolitan Museum of Art. When we were kids, sometimes we would reach up to the top of the closet to look at and try on all of those crazy hats. This time, so many years later, when we went to take the hatboxes down, everything just fell apart in our hands. Sadly, all the hats had to be thrown out. She had dresses and jewelry she had never worn, and purses she had never used. It was like excavating a life that had never been fully lived.

My brother and I debated what to do with all of our stuff that was still there: our Ratfink and Troll collection, all of our comic books, Mad magazines, NY magazines (from the first issue), and all of the painting and drawings I had done over the years at my mother's request. Would the Met want any of this? Nah. We threw out as much as we could.

Bags and bags went down the apartment incinerator chute. It was pee-in-your-pants funny to hear curse words in Spanish from the superintendent echoing through the two floors below as we poured more and more stuff down the chute. Everything salvageable went to Goodwill or to the Salvation Army.

Eighty years of life was reduced to five or six boxes that were stamped with *right side up* when they shipped to LA.

My mother lived for two years in LA and was well enough

for some of that time to enjoy her new apartment, and to hold her newest granddaughter. Mom watched her four-year-old-granddaughter repeatedly crawl into her sister's crib to chew on her ear and do everything she could to make her laugh.

I now have all of the stuff that was important to our mother. I can think of only one thing that we missed, which I wished that we had taken. Hanging on the wall in our kitchen above a broken radio that my brother had promised our mother he'd one day fix, was a decorative plate with the inscription, "G-d bless this lousy apartment." I don't know how we ever left that behind.

I never found my easy bake oven.

WOOF

Like most parents, there is almost nothing we wouldn't do for our precious little ones. Need a purple butterfly suit, no problem, need a kidney, no problem, need a sibling, we'll get right on it, need a dog . . . hold your horses.

When you become a parent you really begin to deeply understand the *give and take* in life, especially the give part. Like most parents, we joyfully lavished our time, attention, and resources to make certain our little creature was happy.

I was thirty-six when our daughter was born. My first memory was of her matchstick little finger wagging in my face. My bundle of joy was very determined and strong willed. At about three, she began to advocate for a sibling. Where did she get this idea? I began to suspect those subversive Teletubbies. I liked Tinky-Winky, especially because he so popped Jerry Falwell's buttons, but I was never quite sure of Dipsy. At any rate, weren't we enough? Didn't most kids want to be the one and only? Evidently, she did not. I/ we thought this might go away in time, or if we changed her viewing habits, but this incessant drumbeat only got more pronounced with her telling all who would listen that she was going to have a sister.

I was not a young mother and had a very busy and demanding job. I will distract her with less TV and more fresh air: I'll take her more often to her favorite place, the tire-wheel park (it had one of those tire rope swings). She had loads of fun there and ate a lot of ice cream, but for her the sister beat did not lessen. I was with my mother who was visiting from NY, on one of those chocolate and vanilla swirl filled days at the park. After a couple hours of play in the sandbox, I thought it was time for us to put our shoes back on and get the hell out of there.

My daughter refused to leave, but not like just any kid who did not want all of that fun playtime to end, she was not budging until I promised to get her a sister. It was an epic standoff, with her literally standing barefoot on a park table and me looking straight into her eyes and saying, "Put your shoes on, we'll talk about this later." She would not move off the table or her position. My mother was amused and muttered under her breath, "Paybacks a bitch." I was not so amused nor was I about to let a three-foot-tall, skinny kid with a mound of curly blonde hair and an opinion, likely influenced by Dipsy, push me around no matter how cute she was and how much I loved her.

There were four years separating her and her sister. Her sister was my fortieth birthday present. I cannot imagine my/our lives, had this kid not shown up. I have a pretty good sense of where my firstborn came from, but her sister is more of a mystery. She was an easy baby who unfolded as a sensitive, kind, compassionate, little girl. So many people went out of their way to comment on her gentle nature. Example: what kid thanks their parent for buying food when standing in line at the grocery? This was a kid who was hardwired to *the give* part of the *give and take* equation.

Life went on, time passed. Everything was quite pleasant and manageable until one day when a five-word question from my sweet little daughter rocked my world: "**Can we get a dog?**"

All of her friends seemed to have one, or be planning to get one, except us. She loved animals, dogs in particular. Everyone in my house seemed willing, except me. So that you don't hate me and stop reading, let me swim out to this wave. I like dogs, I didn't say love, but I like them. Here is my issue: unlike their feline four-legged domestic companions who are happy to be left alone, dogs/puppies require a lot of time and attention. At that time in my life I had a great deal going on including unusual family responsibilities that often required that I be away for long periods of time. What's that expression, *I need an X, like I need a hole in my head?* Here, X equals *woof woof.* Who would care for Lassie? Dino? Benji? Scooby? Whomever?

My firstborn quickly passed through the *I want a doggie phase* my little one did not. My solution was not exactly a puppy substitute. "How would you like to offer a loving home to a few needy fish?" I am pure evil. She was characteristically thankful, and doted on them every day when she got up, and after she got home from school.

Things were ok in the animal kingdom for a while. But every time I turned around some other kid in the neighborhood or from her friend circle was getting a puppy. Naturally, I thought this was yet another conspiracy to make me look bad. Then when I didn't think things could get any worse, my eighty-something-year-old father and stepmother announced that they were getting a puppy. *Et tu Brute?* My own father piled onto the growing heap of guilt I began to amass. My little one was having a hard time with the fact that now seemingly the whole world, including her grandparents, had a mutt, save her.

I had a trip planned to NY where I would soon see my father and the new addition to the family. I promised I would take pictures and call my little daughter as soon as I saw the new pup. When I left, I wasn't sure if the big chunky tears welling up in her eyes were because she wouldn't see me for a few days or she that was puppy-less. I was in the doghouse and felt like crap.

At my dad's house, a little, cute, hyper ball of white fluff greeted me. True to my word, I took a few pictures emailed them and then called home. This puppy love was tiring. The conversation went as follows:

Husband: "How is everybody?"

Me: "Fine." (Barking in the background)

Husband: "What kind of dog is it?"

Me: "A shiatsu?"

Husband: "No, that's a massage."

Me: "A ginzu?" (Louder barking in background)

Husband: "No, that's a knife."

Me: "I don't know. It's some fucking cross between a poodle and a . . ."

At that point my little daughter made herself known on the call and proceeded to tell me what kind of dog it was. She was aware of that breed because one of her best friends had one. Of course she did.

I was mortified. Did she hear me swear? Of course she did. I had been trying to curb my mouth.

She got on the phone with her grandparents who were happy to provide every last detail of all the adorable puppy antics.

Where's that power drill?

She was such a good kid who asked for so little. I really did not want to disappoint her. But I knew, considering all that I had in my doggie bowl, that this was the right decision. I had to be responsible and resolute even though it was so hard to say, "No" to that little face.

A couple of months passed with little yapping until one morning when I went into our bathroom and found pictures of cute little puppies pasted to my side of the bathroom mirror. This was a low blow and a very clever tactic—she must have been getting pointers from her sister. During all this puppy mania I had been maturely describing all of the responsibilities of parenthood of a pup, and how they were, like with a child, lifelong.

In this conversation, I found myself saying, "I'd rather adopt a baby." While this became sort of a friends-and-family joke,

I had been giving that notion some thought. Motherhood and the crazy love of kids was a time released, late in life, revelation. Like my firstborn, I was pretty specific. If I did adopt, I wanted an Asian baby girl. One of my daughter's best friends was Japanese/Caucasian and highly adorable. She called me *Mommy #2*, I called her *Daughter #3*. As a cute little Asian baby girl swirl danced through my head, the thought of snickers from the young mommies in the preschool playground popped that little thought bubble.

I needed to maturely respond to my daughter's art project on my bathroom mirror. I put myself in *high ski*m and searched through my T. Berry Brazelton bible, but saw nothing that referenced dogs. Nothing helpful from Dr. Spock either, but I'm not completely fluent in Vulcan. I was on my own. The next morning my little one awoke to pictures of cute little Asian babies on her bathroom mirror.

Even though she was old enough to understand the issues, the heart wants what the heart wants, and she did not give up.

The next bow-wow episode was when I brought the girls to NY to see the family and meet its newest member. She was a tad bigger but no less hyper. While my kids had fun frolicking with the pup, again, I got that sinking feeling: I knew what was coming. Later in that week, I took them into NYC. I needed a break from the barking. It was a beautiful warm summer night. My little one started the conversation, one that I needed to once and for all end.

She: "I promise I will do most of the work, remind you

about vet appointments, walking, and other stuff."

Me: "So you're telling me that you plan to drop out of school or you will just tell the dog to hold it until you return home eight hours later?"

She: "Well, no, I guess you'd have to walk it."

Good, she finally saw that. She also noticed that we had entered an area where all the signs and storefronts were written in Chinese.

She: "Where are we?"

Me: "Chinatown."

She: "Where are we going?"

Me: "We're going to get your new baby sister."

A slight look of panic crossed her face. Then she started to laugh.

We ended up having a delicious meal that night. When I read my fortune cookie out loud it said, "One day you will have a grand-dog." We all came away full (for a few hours) and with more of an understanding of each other's points of view.

It's now been several years. She has tons of friends, interests, activities, and very little time. Someday at the right time, I imagine her being followed by a cute little furry creature on four legs that loves her dearly. I have a suggestion for its name, *Lucky*.

DO I GLOW
IN THE DARK?

Our mother was *high risk* because she had us in what was then considered old age: forty-one. Hospitals and doctors handled a high-risk pregnancy in the 1950s differently than now. She was given large amounts of a popular drug, DES. I was hoping that this referred to Discrete Event Simulation—it did not. *It* was Diethylstilbestrol, which was first given to pregnant women during the late 1940s until the mid 1970s to prevent miscarriages (it was used for other conditions as well). Over two million women took DES during this time period.

I was told about DES early in life and thought I would do some homework. My initial observation was the first three letters of the clinical/chemical name, **DIE**. This was not a good sign. From reading all that I could at the time, I arrived at a simple conclusion: I was fucked—along with everyone else exposed to DES with the possible exception of the lawyers, who busily prepared class action lawsuits against the drug companies that thought pumping high doses of a synthetic estrogen into expecting mothers and developing fetuses was a good idea. Back then, at twenty-five cents a pop, the drug companies made piles of money and only stopped selling DES after a few lawyers pointed out that it was both harmful and ineffective. And, oh yes, it seemed that at least one company had this knowledge prior to selling the drug . . . must watch out for those pesky paper trails.

Suffice it to say, this *exposure* gave me more exposure to medical and biological research than I cared to have. This, however, would only be the tip of the iceberg; later in life I would go on to do much more research and ask many questions to countless doctors and scientists. But after my initial foray into the Life Science world, I tucked all this fascinating information away and got back to the subject that most interested me: having fun.

Almost twenty years later, and after much *fun* was had, the phone rang and it did not bring good news. This is when the *fun* stopped and it happened, like it does for so many, in an instant.

My twin was experiencing some very funky things that we later discovered involved some foreign matter on his brain stem. I had a pretty good idea of the brain's location thanks to the Scarecrow, but I was clueless about its operation. Thus began my renewed interest in all things biomedical. Finding the cause of my bother's sudden illness and *fixing* it took over my life as his illness slowly, very slowly, claimed his.

When my brother became acutely symptomatic, his doctor was convinced that he had only a touch of Vertigo. He gave him Antivert and sent him on his way. Several weeks passed with no real relief. I insisted that he go back and ask for an MRI. I will never forget the response from that doctor, "I can take a picture, but I guarantee we won't find anything." I had many questions for this doctor; none of which were ever adequately answered. It took that doctor almost three months to admit his diagnosis may not have been the correct one and for him to refer my brother to a neurologist. The first thing the neurologist did was to take a *picture*. A few weeks later, my brother underwent a biopsy to gain further insight into a clearly visible mass on his MRI. He was immediately put on high doses of Prednisone, but it was late in the disease process.

Nothing could give back what time had taken, but as we went forward, I did my best to make certain that the last person the original arrogant *doctor* would ever misdiagnose was my brother. Under threat of a lawsuit, he eventually resigned his practice.

My brother had a rare presentation of a rare neurological disease. His case was serious and complex with symptoms and complications that emerged over time and confounded the many other doctors we saw. After months playing *Stump the Doctor* all across the country, my brother and I met a doctor in LA who stood out and above the crowd and for so many reasons. Ultimately, he was the one doctor willing to *call* my brother's diagnosis. After several months in his care, my brother went back to his home in CT to continue his treatment. We were both hopeful.

In addition to providing the roadmap for my brother's treatment plan, this same doctor inspired me to think about the origin of disease. It occurred to me that one could not understand how things go wrong unless one had the knowledge of how the body was originally designed to work. I began to read about stem cells, systems biology, and many related subjects. I was highly motivated to learn the *operating system* of human life. If so, then maybe it would be possible to help my brother repair the damage that had been done so that he could someday resume his happy life. This shouldn't be too tough.

Over time, my office looked like that of a hyper-focused, bordering on crazy-ass, obsessed detective hunting a serial killer on any number of countless TV cop shows.

Late at night, when delirium set in, I often fantasized about getting all the great science and tech minds in the world together. They would meet at a lovely resort in a temperate climate, like perhaps where the folks who worked on the Manhattan project hung out, so that more answers to big questions could be found. Of course, I would be there to ask a lot of questions, bother some, amuse others, and maybe even offer something of value . . . or maybe not.

During the years of my research, and as it related to my brother's case, I did come to some very definite conclusions, and while they may never be one hundred percent factually proven, I believe the origin of his very rare and complex medical issue stemmed from his exposure to DES. I presented my theory and evidence to that very smart and special doctor who patiently listened and thought that my hypothesis was indeed plausible. At the conclusion of that conversation, he asked if I would be interested in attending the medical school where he taught. He was being serious, and, while I was remarkably touched by his offer, I quickly determined that spending the next twelve years studying until *I* was able to say to someone, *follow my finger* would not bring much added benefit to anyone. I would have to find another way to make a contribution.

Instead, in tandem with my self-taught faux MD/Ph.D., I spent several years helping to raise money for, and awareness of, various science programs at a stem cell center of a local University. I also busied myself by thinking about how technology could be more effectively applied to healthcare. I became slightly obsessed with the idea of developing an *OnStar* system for humans. This kept me busy for several years. The most daunting obstacle I discovered: our bodies are much more sophisticated than any technology yet developed.

Most importantly for me, I used the information I acquired over the nine years of my brother's illness to inform him of all of the progress being made on the cutting edge in science and in medicine. My brother enjoyed hearing about all this, and when he was still able to speak, often joked that his illness and my homework assignments probably saved me from having developed brain rot. Likely so. In addition,

I was very active in monitoring my brother's care. At times, this created friction with a few of his doctors . . . ok, maybe more than a few. Overall, my brother was fortunate to have had many health care professionals who were truly outstanding practitioners and compassionate human beings.

Do I glow in the dark? That was the question I would often ask my brother late at night in his nursing home when I would turn down the lights before I left. Even in all that darkness I could see his smile.

It's been several years since my brother passed away and because I have two girls who I am quite fond of, I continue to read about science, now with an emphasis on Epigenetics. Simply, Epigenetics is the study of how, over time, external influences affect and/or alter one's DNA. Example: *Will, or how will, my DES exposures affect my kids and my grandbabies?* Long-term studies suggest that it might.

So with all this *homework* what can I pass on? There are internal and external factors that affect one's health. The former is hard-wired and is therefore a challenge to predict or control. The latter affects the former, allowing for some control; in other words: what you put into your body matters: drugs (FDA and other), food, blah, blah, blah.

Oh yeah, one last comment: don't be afraid to ask doctors questions; the good ones won't mind.

PROVIDENCE

I've had a running conversation with a life-long friend about fate and destiny; about how they are distinct and often in conflict. It can be confusing. Generally, I've had pretty good instincts about all this, which is a good thing since I live life with a Welcome mat out for when fate comes knockin'.

I was in an airport and my flight was delayed for hours. I can't even recall where I was going or why. I do remember that I had a can of peanuts that had been given to me for my upcoming journey. I passed the time talking to a group of very delightful college students who gobbled up the nuts like monkeys at the zoo.

Finally, when we I boarded, I noticed another small group of animals that obviously passed the time waiting at some watering hole; they were drunk off their asses. As long as they weren't wearing a pilot uniform, I really couldn't care less. I boarded the plane and settled into my window seat. Soon after, the aisle seat in my row was occupied leaving only the middle seat that I hoped would be for *Elijah*.

The small group of loud asses was now on the plane. I looked up and my eyes locked onto one in the herd who alternated between looking at me and his boarding pass.

Then in a voice more appropriate for a sports event he seemed to feel the necessity to bellow, "Yeah . . . this must be my lucky day!" I had the exact opposite reaction. As he climbed into his seat, I quickly reached for my airsick bag, and put it on my lap in hopes that he would find another seat (this was a handy little trick I learned from a friend who swore it worked every time). He looked at the bag and without missing a beat said, "Ah, don't worry honey, I'm not going to be sick." Just like a man. How long was this flight?

I was a veteran traveler and had many chance encounters. I usually enjoyed these experiences. I don't know what it is about planes and trains; often people feel unbound and ready to share some pretty intimate details of their lives. Maybe it's the altitude or the speed? Anyway, I was in no mood for this.

I had long carried a *Get Out of Jail Free* card in my wallet; where was that *Do Not Disturb* sign? I began the search for my Altoids. He was leaning into me insistent upon exhibiting both his bad breath and behavior. The fire demanded a fire line: be in my face, I'll be in yours. "So, I notice that gold ring you're wearing, do you have a family as well as a wife?" "Oh, you do . . . how about that. Any girls? Oh, you do . . . how about that. And if one of them sat next to a drunken dumb ass like yourself, who was as forward as you are with me, how do you suppose you'd react?" "I'd pop the guy in the face" he responded after a brief pause. "Well, don't let *me* hold you back."

This seemed to quiet him down, and after a few minutes

of silence, he apologized. More time passed, and, after a cup of coffee, he began a civil and appropriate conversation that evolved into more of a therapy session—his not mine. "I could learn a lot from you," he said in earnest. He began to discuss his marriage, its difficulties, and the disappointments he felt. We discussed little things like how communication works, perspective, and how it was good to have it and to be able to take others into consideration—blah, blah, blah. He seemed to be a guy who might have a shot at redemption. I refer to those men as **temporarily** emotionally disabled rather than permanently disabled (for a fun and free gift for your own special idiot, please visit www.ileighprivate.com to obtain a special sign to help identify your emotionally disabled man).

The plane had finally landed. My plane neighbor was sober, serious, and sensitized. "Ok, lets wrap this up. You love your wife; go home and say it BECAUSE you mean it; not LIKE you mean it." We shook hands when we parted.

Ultimately, I was glad that our lives crossed. He headed home to fine tune his destiny. I was en route to my next appointment and, by that time, I was hungry and wished I had those peanuts.

Much earlier in life, when I was on my self-directed term abroad, I had a much more significant chance encounter: one that altered my plans and the course of many lives. My best friend and I were traveling together, when, in mid-trip, we mutually decided to change our plans: I would stay in Europe and she would travel to Israel. Our itinerary originally had us working for a month on a kibbutz. Now, because of this change in plans, she chose to go to a different kibbutz. There she met a man who would later become her husband . . . fate and destiny merging in harmony (they are still happily together). While she toiled in her kibbutz and played *getting to know you* with her new love, I was on a train leaving from Barcelona heading to Madrid.

I was a happy little idiot clutching my *Lets Go* book, trying to determine where I'd stay when I got off the train. When I boarded the train, I passed a cute but very scruffy looking guy with a big duffle bag and took my seat several rows away. The train quickly filled, and I had company: a paunchy middle-aged man who thought it was ok to harass me by pointing to pictures in a porn magazine. This harassment crescendoed when he put his hand on my knee and began to move it up my thigh. I was terrified, speechless, and likely in shock. It was at this point when the young man that I had passed came to my rescue and confronted the psycho pervert.

Their heated exchange of words went from zero to sixty in no time, and yet, in what seemed like slow motion, my knight in shining armor was on top of the other man, uncontrollably beating the life out of him. Blood splattered everywhere. People screamed and moved away from the unfolding drama as the train began to slow. I was shaking my knight and pleading with him to stop. He got up, looked at me as if we had forever known each other and softly whispered, "Let's go." This was not the *Let's Go* that

I had known and come to rely upon. My instinct rose and led; the rest of me followed.

I grabbed my backpack and started to run to the train door along with my blood-splattered madman-knight. I don't know what possessed me to jump off of the train as it slowed to a stop and follow this young man, but I did.

This was the beginning of an extraordinary journey together: much of it spent in Paris, since he had no affection for the country we had just left, the one that had hosted him to three years in one of its prisons for a drug related crime with which he swore he had no involvement. His was an epic story of love, betrayal, of fate wrestling with destiny, and it was now one that somehow included me.

I thought I had knowledge and experience enough, but nothing in my twenty years prepared me for this. Yet, there I was, fated to help this person find his way back to life—to find his way back home.

After three weeks of slowly peeling away the layers of emotional dirt and grime from my new friend, we parted in a moment as seemingly random as the one that brought us together. I had a good sense of fate's plan, and while it was difficult for us to part, it was necessary.

A year passed when I next heard from him. I received a letter that included a picture. He was with the young family he had left behind before *no good* took him on a strange detour from his destiny.

There are so many possible connections and interactions among people. When you turn a corner and bump into someone, it's hard to know how it will all play out. I continue to rely upon instinct, good judgment, and providence.

And, oh yeah, it never hurts to have some Altoids on hand.

VISITING THE POT
APOTHECARY

I have tried everything to help me fall and stay asleep including varying types and degrees of alcohol, homeopathic, and FDA regulated remedies. I've rocked in a hammock wearing earplugs and a blindfold. I've tried sound therapy (Buddhist and Gregorian chants, bird chirping, waves crashing). I've had *regular therapy* (whatever that is) and NOTHING really provided lasting relief.

Destiny intervened when my daughter decided to *fix* her split ends. While I told my tale of sleepless woe to my former hairdresser, he first correlated the time of my depravity with when I left him and then offered a two-word solution, "smoke weed." Since he was an expert on all things head related, I thought I'd give his suggestion serious consideration.

I hadn't smoked pot since President Bill was in office and only on the occasional Friday night after the end of a long production week. Like with cigarettes, I used to grub joints, preferring to believe that I had only a passive and occasional relationship with both. I had not actually bought pot since around the time *the clapper* was introduced. I only remembered this because it was a late night pot inspired purchase.

Another flashback to, um I mean memory, of a pot induced consumer product purchase springs to mind: we held a Tupperware party at college. A lovely woman from our local community arrived to demonstrate the latest products offered. She represented Tupperware, and we represented Mars. It was a very amusing night. We bought quite a bit of Tupperware, and at times, we even used some of it. During the quiet of the library, that oh so familiar burping sound could be heard. Tupperware was a sound investment in our entertainment.

Flash forward to my sleepless nights.

Luckily for me, I live in the great and progressive state of CA where many medical pot dispensaries exist. Abbott Kinney is a street in Venice that is terminally hip: a good place for the right kind of Rite-Aid. The medical dispensary there often caught my attention, but I never ventured into it. Now, I was on a mission. I put on my very best pair of beaten-to-shit boots and hipster attitude and crossed the border into the imagined kingdom of *The Farmacy*.

It was not the run-of-the-mill Venice head shop that one would expect to see at the beach. Sam Walton would have been proud; a friendly greeter met me at the door and directed me to a lovely young girl behind the counter of an immaculate and well-stocked store. Trying to break the tension (my own) and doing my best to channel Jack Webb,

I said the following: "I'd like to purchase a Marijuana ciga-rette." She did not pick up the reference. I quickly recovered by launching into my tale of menopause-induced sleepless-ness hoping that she might have a mom experiencing the same kind of issues. She was a total professional.

I received quite the education: over one hundred differ-ent *medicines* with several different *delivery systems*. Wow, *delivery systems*; the roach had obviously learned a lot from La Roche. There was much to consider: I had only known of two types of pot, pot for *everyday*, Mexican, and pot for *nice*, Hawaiian. The lecture on delivery options included: a soda-like beverage (clearly the choice of the newest gen-eration), edibles, even eye drops. If I wanted to smoke, a vaporizer was suggested. "I'm old school, rolling papers or a pipe will do."

As all this transpired, I could not help but notice the *phar-macist* who stood perched on a platform behind us. He was completely absorbed by what he was doing and had a huge smile on his face. If we were truly in the magic kingdom and the scene was animated, he would be the cat who ate the canary. He looked so high. My helpful young woman's next question brought me quickly back to live action: *"Do you have a prescription?"* *"Well . . ."*

A few days before the magic kingdom, I had an appoint-ment with my gastroenterologist who had over the years shared her own sleepless in LA stories with me. I've always believed that it was a good thing to find some common ground with someone who is sticking his or her finger up your ass. I mentioned my planned visit to the pot store thinking that, perchance, she might be inclined to write a prescription, which I thought I might need. Think again. However, she did ask me to let her know if I found some relief after I tried it.

Back at The Farmacy, *Momma's little helper* handed me a card with an address where, for forty-five dollars, I could have a consultation with a *doctor* who could provide me the necessary prescription. I was totally suspect. What doctor on the Westside of LA charges forty-five dollars for services rendered? Thank G-d it was 2013 and I was only there for some pot and not 1970 and in need of an abortion. I noticed that the *doctor* was near Costco. I would go the next time I needed to stop for a year's supply of anything—I'm a mommy: always multi-tasking.

Later that week, I recounted my story to a friend and fellow mommy. She quickly offered to help by becoming my supplier. "I'll let you know when the next shipment is available." I always admired her enterprising *can do* spirit from when we both ran our kid's elementary school fundraiser. I received a text from her a few days' later during Rosh Hashanah services: I viewed this as a sign.

We soon met and she gave me my stash. "Great. Any rolling paper?" "Try the Mobile station on the corner." Oh happy day, yet another step. I walked out of the gas station with a Slim Jim, a power-ball ticket, and a packet of Zig-Zag rolling papers, which, at $2.50 a pack seemed like a bargain. I was pleased to learn that inflation had not done to rolling paper what it did to gas.

Rolling a joint was not like riding a bike. I fondly recalled my hand crafted pipe from high school, it was the face of Richard Nixon, with his open mouth serving as the bowl. I wondered where it was and if I could get it refurbished.

Dinner that night seemed interminable. I could not wait for a reasonable time to announce my bedtime. Nine thirty seemed reasonable. By nine forty I was standing on my upstairs toilet blowing smoke out of the bathroom window so that my teenage daughter would not detect any evidence of my new sleep aid.

I went to bed and proceeded to bounce, or zig-zag, from one distant crack in my brain to another. Endless contemplation was not the desired effect. I was up for hours. At about four thirty, I returned to my tried and true friend, Mr. Xanax, for a few hours of sleep. That morning I decided to go to Costco for one thousand rolls of toilet paper, a ten-gallon container of ketchup . . . and while in the area, a visit to *the doctor*.

I found a parking space directly in front of the *doctor's* storefront office. A woman at the reception desk seemed like she was doing me a favor to look up and acknowledge me. She handed me a six-page health questionnaire to complete. What? Are you for real? "Is this really necessary?" From her nasty stare, I determined that it was. I briefly considered creating an alias, but then reconsidered as she seemed humorless and had my Drivers license. I sat down in the waiting room and began to fill out my heath profile surrounded by stacks of *Golf* and *Architectural Digest* magazines; they were somewhat comforting. I expected to catch the latest issue of *High Times*.

I politely handed her back all of the paperwork while inwardly reciting the mantra I use when I encounter people like her, "You can kill more bees with honey . . . you fucking bitch." "I'll call you when the doctor is ready to see you." A minute later, she called my name and lead me into the examination room where she sternly told me to sit on the exam table that had on it the standard blue paper gown. "Um, not to be uncooperative here, but . . . there's no way I'm taking my clothes off for a gram of pot." Before she could say anything, or kick me, in walked the doctor.

He looked like he could have been my father. Thankfully, he was not. "I too have sleep issues, but I've never tried pot, ever." He had a nice smile and a twinkle in his eye. I liked him immediately. As he took my blood pressure, he asked a few questions. Then it was my turn: "How did you get into this line of work?" He was retired, looking for something to do and missed meeting and talking with people. A half hour later, and only after I mentioned my parking meter and how I seemed to be a magnet for meter maids (oh, pardon me, Parking Enforcement Officers), was I able to extricate myself from his office. He would not let me go without the promise to come back and let him know if pot really helped my sleeplessness. He handed me my prescription, which was good for a year.

On my way out, I remembered to retrieve my Drivers

license from the charming woman who eye-rolled me as she handed back my license. I wondered, what's the opposite of receptionist?

Mercifully, I didn't get a ticket. I didn't have much time before I had to pick up my daughter from school. I passed Costco and headed directly to The Farmacy.

Prescription in hand, I walked in and was warmly greeted by no fewer than three people offering their help. I went through my song and dance, as did they: no buying for other people, legal in CA, not with the Feds blah, blah, blah. Dang, you mean I can't start selling this to my fifteen-year-old and all her friends? Dang. Next, they handed me a two-page *menu*. Not having my glasses, I defaulted to my standard refrain when given a menu, "What do you recommend?" She thoughtfully paused and then suggested I try, *GRAVEYARD*. "I want to go to sleep, but not for that long." We were both laughing, which seemed to have a multiplier effect as everyone in the store joined in with our little chuckle . . . of course they would.

After we all regained our composure, she showed me the quality of the material, or buds, and then asked if I had a *grinder*—"yeah, for coffee." One of her co-workers graciously ground my buds. I began to believe that Venice, not Anaheim, was the happiest place on earth." I left with a twenty-dollar gram of Graveyard.

It is now day three of my little experiment. Graveyard has proven to be very relaxing, and it does help me to fall asleep. Staying asleep . . . well that's another story.

FACE TIME

I had been taking art lessons from a sweet old French woman for about two years when my mother handed me a photograph of a little girl ripped from the pages of National Geographic magazine and said, "Paint this. She looks just like you did when you were this age"(she looked to be five). Not wanting to disappoint my mother, I said, "Ok."

I took the photograph to my art teacher, stretched a canvas, and got to work. I spent hours looking at the picture before lifting a piece of charcoal to make a mark. For some reason I was not in a rush. It took months before I finally declared the painting finished, and by that time I had also decided that this painting would be my last. I was fourteen when I said good-bye to my painting teacher. Then I brought the picture home to my mother; she framed it and then hung it up in our apartment, where it remained for almost thirty years, until I inherited it from her after she passed.

My youngest daughter, daughter #2, was around five when she came home from kindergarten with a photograph her teacher had taken of her while she played in the school-yard. Something about that picture stopped me; it was the same face, haircut, and pose of the little girl my mother made me paint so long ago. The resemblance was remarkable. I put the snapshot next to the painting, shrugged, and went on my way.

Five years later, I was hiking through remote villages in Bhutan with my lucky little fourteen-year-old daughter, daughter number one. I could hear her cursing me under her breath as we made our way up and down many mountains that day. We stopped at a village where she went off with others on our tour for a late afternoon snack and a break from me.

I found myself wandering around with my camera until I came upon a little girl playing in her front yard. She looked to be about five. I stopped, we exchanged greetings, and then we just looked at each other holding that stare for a few beats longer than one might expect. She looked so familiar. After about a half hour of talking and playing in her yard, I took a picture of my new little friend. Then sadly, it was time to leave, and we had to say good-bye.

I caught up with the group and joined them on the bus that would take us to our hotel for a much deserved evening rest. While on the bus I looked at the picture that I took of my Bhutanese little girl. It and she were so beautiful; she filled the frame with joy. I proudly passed the camera to our tour leader, "Look at her, look at the picture I just took . . ." He glanced at the back of my camera, smiled, and then said, "You didn't take it she *gave* it to you." Ok, I'll go with that.

Months after the trip, my Bhutanese little girl was still on my mind. I never print pictures, but I decided to print her picture. There she was: so big, so real, and so beautiful. I put her picture adjacent to the one I painted and the photo of my youngest daughter. I just stood there captured by all three pictures arranged together. All the subjects in the images shared the same face, the same haircut, and the same pose.

I sent a print of the picture I *was given* of my Bhutanese angel to my tour director in Bhutan. I wanted him to find her. I wanted her to have it. I never found out if she received it.

To this day, and each day that passes, I begin mine by looking at all three of those faces.

Someday I will go back, maybe when my little Bhutanese friend is fourteen or so. I know I will find her. I know I will recognize her . . . I'd know that face anywhere.

VIXEN

Ain't nothing like the real thing, girl groups, to help one withstand the ocean's tides when life's little undercurrents, gentle waves, and fucking tsunamis threaten to pull you under or wash you away. I am lucky; I have many such circles of friends, and fabulous Singlettes from various times in life. These are girls who have your back rather than talk behind it, girls who are without judgment, girls who have soul, and girls who like to Go-Go(s) and have some fun.

In the early days of one such group, we met at a local Chinese restaurant. It must have been frightening; twenty women all with grade school kids ready for a night out. We had several rounds of drinks before we ordered dinner. The waiters were all huddled together afraid of coming near us; likely all of them bobbed their heads in agreement over why sex-selective abortions were once so popular back in the homeland. The Girls Aloud were raucous. But, we did leave a good tip. From that outing, we formed the core group of five founding members of *The Mommy Martini Club*.

Since then, this little group of Runaways has gone on

many adventures to various spa and resort locations. It was not all poolside partying, mud baths, dining out, and martini miniature golf outings. I think we may have attended a cultural event once, but I'm not sure. Our conversations are broad and in depth on topics such as nuclear disarmament, deficit reduction, global warming; oh, I'm sorry, wrong group. We almost always talk and laugh about relationships. Husbands/boyfriends and relationship status are big topics along with exercise, sleep and whatever's En Vogue. It's like Cosmo coming to life for this little group of Spice Girls. You don't *really* think we trade recipes do you?

In the many years since this group's formation, and as we *age up*, life's little ripples have directed the conversation to various challenges we, and our families, have faced: kid issues, near-empty nests, *second acts*, the balance of work and play, aging parents, the *Seven Year Bitch*, and, the now ever so popular, *who turned the heat up?* (Also known as crazy fucking hormones). We talk about fears, real and imagined, and what holds us back. It is during these times we recognize, and deeply appreciate, that it is us who holds us up when life conspires to bring us down.

Life provides so many wonderful *back-up* singers.

Other little Bangles of girls have adorned and graced my life, and although the diaspora has hit, we make a big effort to frequently come together. After all, sisterhood is the motherload of invention. These reunions often involve our kids, and, magically, like Destiny's Child, all happen to be girls. Ah, the next generation of Little Mix, they rein Supreme(s).

I could not imagine the world without these Dreamgirls, it just wouldn't sound right.

"SHE'S MY DAUGHTER, SHE'S MY SISTER . . ."

Life can be very confusing when it comes to having a career and being a mommy. I knew from when I was really little that I was different than many of my other female playmates. They wanted to play with *Barbie*; I wanted to play with an atom smasher. I had the good fortune to use that line many, many years later with Barbie's mom, Ruth Handler. I spent months unsuccessfully groveling for the film rights to her book, *Dream Doll*. She was a trailblazing visionary who made all girls fixate on their breasts. Years later, when she lost her own to cancer, and no suitable replacement alternatives existed, she started yet another company to address this problem.

Most interesting to me, her story epitomized the inherent conflict in *having it all and doing it all* as a businesswoman and a mom. Her great success had come at a cost.

Ultimately, she decided not to broadcast her life or her family's life to millions. Professionally, I was disappointed with her decision because I so badly wanted to make this movie. As a mom, I totally understood her concerns and respected her decision. Although I have met many extraordinary and accomplished people in my little career, my lunches with Ruth Handler were a highlight and inspiration to me. Her story made me think deeply about my life choices and my role as a *Mom*.

On my daughter's first day at Nursery school, I was pretty darned surprised to find that I was in the minority because I was a working mommy. The majority of mommies elected to, or had the ability to be, full time stay-at-home moms. Several of these women had given up significant positions and careers to do so—to each his or her own.

I did experience occasional pangs of insecurity and guilt when I knew all those other mommies were in school with their little devils sitting on their laps while my daughter was not. At that point in my life it was unimaginable to me to give up the career I somehow managed to engineer. I was running a television production company and even though my odds of producing a hit show were about as good as winning the lotto, I loved my job and was not planning to give it up anytime soon. We had a great nanny, and our progeny seemed happy and well adjusted. Then, as time passed, things began to change.

Over the years, my job became increasingly frustrating,

and my personal life became more complicated. I had another kid on the way and a mother who began to lose her way having many complex health issues. The delicate dance that once seemed so effortless was not so any longer. After sixteen years of non-stop work, I needed to hit the pause button, focus on the home front, and recharge my battery. My job ended and for the first time in my life, I had no plans to venture anywhere outside of the playground and the supermarket. This did not last long.

Old habits die-hard; lunch is a hard thing to give up in this town. It wasn't long before I was *doing lunch* with various people: one who had a nifty idea with great potential for an Internet marketing venture.

I partnered with this person and took the leadership role in its development. I was in start-up land. What was I thinking? That *push-pull* began again in full force, only this time without any real physical division in work/home space and, by then, with two little ones, my sick mother, and nanny underfoot. After almost a year developing this venture, the stock market crashed (the dot-com bomb) along with any hope for the long term financing necessary to make that venture viable. I had pulled my former employer, a big ad agency, into this project, and together we thought it best to put it on the back burner until market conditions were more favorable.

Interestingly, while most lamented the market crash, I felt a sense of calm and relief. I had more than a few difficult moments with my little ones when they could not understand why *mommy* was home and yet unavailable to them. I could not stand to see *little miss pigtails* with big chunky tears as she left with our nanny for the playground. When push came to shove, I realized that I wanted that job, and so, I went for it.

I went deep into Mommy-land. I became more involved in school activities, learned how to use the appliances in our kitchen, and involved myself in various at-home activities like deciding to GC (general contract) the building of our pool. Hey, I've produced TV shows—it's all very analogous, right? After twice the normal time, and let's not discuss the cost overages, I did manage to get the pool done without flooding the neighborhood, just my own backyard.

My new *at home job* was an eye opener, with all kinds of work and challenges; all of which I happily embraced. I loved opening the front door and having a bus load of kids fly into my house, and I got a tremendous amount of pleasure from the endless hours of being lifeguard at our pool. Whenever I had to fill out a form that *defined me*, now instead of writing *television or advertising executive*, I simply wrote, "Mommy." I didn't like the *homemaker* label; it felt dated and maybe a bit pejorative. Ok, maybe I'm being a bit too defensive here. Simply put: I loved being with my kids and their friends. I wore my mommy badge with honor. My new best line was: "I'm just like the LA cops: 'Protect and Serve.'"

As proud as I was of my title, I began to notice that others didn't seem to place as much value on it. Surprisingly, many of those to which I refer were women. This was pretty disturbing, and it smacked me in the face one day after a lovely field trip. After an extensive daylong excursion to Sea World with the kids, a fellow mommy, and I were in a hotel lobby having a much-deserved drink while the kiddies played upstairs with their babysitter. The other mommy noticed a large cluster of humanity: all of them with nametags and all from my former university; I must have missed that email.

My friend insisted that we go mingle. It was not high on my list of one hundred things to do before I die, but I didn't want to argue, so I waded into the crowd. Before long, I found myself actively engaged in delightful banter with a woman who was a very senior representative of the school. It was quite a fluid and fun conversation *until* she asked me, "And what do you do"(notice the tense, present not past)? I responded, "I'm a mommy." She then just turned and quickly walked away, no "Nice talking to you," she just left. Jeez, that's so rude—Shamu was better behaved. Hadn't her mother taught her anything?

I had graduated from an Ivy League university and ended up a *MOMMY*, what a *fail*—in her eyes. It wasn't my ego that needed validation; I couldn't care less. It was just so disappointing that she dismissed and devalued a *job* so fundamental and of consequence to an individual and to society. A mom is potentially a kid's most important teacher. How could a teacher not see this and place a premium on it—especially one as highly placed and credentialed as she? Correct me if I'm wrong, but the whole notion of *choice* was a long fought battle for women and need we talk about discrimination?

Sadly, this would not be the last time where this inherent contradiction and prejudice surfaced. Women have such complex feelings about the role of motherhood. The next example was a direct hit on home, not just close to it:

In the last two weeks of my mother's life I had yet another illuminating observation about her and how the world imposed pressure and judgment upon a life. She was talking with a nurse trying to subtotal her life by telling this woman all of her many accomplishments: she was a concert pianist, she had a long career in the fashion industry, and she held many significant volunteer positions with important Non-Profit organizations. Nowhere in this soliloquy was mention of her as a mother. It was sad. I have had so many conversations with women on both sides of the aisle on this topic. It truly is such a personal decision.

Many years later, I met with a woman who I greatly admired: a very well respected television executive. Our conversation focused on her new position and the possibility of me having some involvement with it. She said to me very curiously, "Where've you been?" I began to explain my ten-year time out and my decision to be *all in* with family commitments and responsibilities. She seemed to understand, yet, I could not help but think that she was looking at me like I had two heads; one could make that case.

147

I am very grateful and fortunate that I was able to spend the time that I did with my kids during their Wonder Years. For so many mommies, it's not an option. My job at home was a gift. I did what I wanted and needed to do to support my family. Nothing would have altered my decision. And during this time, I had a lot of help and support from my mommy friends: some who worked in offices and others who worked at home.

Generally speaking, we all love and want the same things for our kids. It would be good and way less stressful if we supported and respected one another in the very personal ways in which we determine how best to live our lives regardless of what hats we wear. I think that's why Barbie has all those different outfits, and she looked great in all of them, chesty little bitch.

BLANCHE DUBOIS & THE KINDNESS OF STRANGERS

(Warning: you will not find much comedy below, although, it was far from absent during this time in life. It had its place and did its job during the best and worst in *The Tale of Two Siblings*).

I have been the lucky recipient of so many wonder-filled moments that have served to confirm my belief in the goodness of people. The story of my brother's illness and our journey through it together is too long to tell in this rambling collection of stories, and I'm not even sure if I can ever do it justice. I will share a few moments, among countless others, during this time that left an indelible mark.

The first was when my brother was straddling between this world and the next after spending weeks in an intensive care unit in upstate New York. I was there with him, staying at a nearby bed and breakfast run by two middle-aged hippies, who I affectionately referred to as *Dharma and Greg*. One day, when I arrived at the hospital, I was told that my brother's precarious state was made worse by a very serious sinus infection that had rapidly developed. An ENT (Ear, Nose, and Throat) doctor would be called in to perform what they told me was a delicate operation because of the severity of the infection and the location of the sinuses involved.

After the usual salutations when we first met, the ENT simply said, "Tell me about your brother." Like a trained seal, I immediately launched into my brother's current status and medical history in intricate detail. This, however, was not the information this doctor wanted from me.

He stopped me and said, "No, tell me about your brother, the person. I like to know about the person who I am about to operate on." I was completely taken aback. My brother had countless doctors parachuting into his case. None of his doctors had this request and sincere level of interest. Where could I begin? I knew this doctor did not have hours or days for me.

I tried to give him my brother's *crib notes*: who he was and how much he meant to me and to so many. When I stopped, the ENT put his arms around me and said that he would do his very best to bring him safely back to me and to those who loved him. I was very touched by his humanity.

He was a man of his word. The operation was long but the outcome was a success. After the operation, I thanked him and then I watched him as he walked down a long corridor never to see or speak with him again.

My next *moment* occurred years later during the time my brother was in a nursing home in Flushing, NY. This would be his last *home*, ironically only miles away from where we spent the first five years of our lives. On one particular day, after several during which I was completely uncertain as to whether my brother even knew if I was there, I decided to go out for a walk. I did this on most days there, but the walks were usually short excursions sometimes only around the corner for a midday break, tea or a savory meal in one of the many Korean restaurants in the area.

On this day, I needed more time. I was feeling as low to the ground as one could get without cracking the pavement. My brother had spent the past year in a regular rotation between the hospital and his nursing home. By then, his breathing was courtesy of Siemens; he was on a ventilator and had been for over two years. At times, when he was awake and alert, I'd ask him in our own way, if he wanted to *go o*n. He always nodded or mouthed, "yes."

After a recent stint in the hospital, I ran into his neurologist who hadn't seen him in some time because his issues were no longer neurological per se; they were medical—effects from having had his disease. He was surprised that my brother was still alive. He then said to me "There is no medical explanation for your brother; we're in G-d territory."

It was getting harder and harder for me to justify my

decision to support my brother's wishes and to stay out of the action between him and the big HIM. All of this was swirling around in my head as I headed out on that cold winter's day.

I walked into many new neighborhoods with city sounds and teaming masses surrounding me. After an hour of aimlessly roaming, my friend, despair, and me, decided we were hungry.

We crossed the street and entered a very small and narrow Chinese restaurant. No one spoke English. I pointed to a picture of soup and sat down at one of the three tables. I was looking down at the table waiting for my soup to arrive when faint baby sounds caught my attention. I looked up to see sitting at the back table, a young mother and her very tiny baby nestled in her arms. I didn't want to stare, but I just couldn't take my eyes off of them. She smiled and I returned the gesture before resuming my table inspection.

Within moments, I felt a presence over me and assumed my soup had arrived. When I looked up, it was the young mother. She was holding her arms out offering me her baby. She did not speak English, and I did not speak Chinese. I tried to politely decline; it was so spontaneous and unusual. She insisted. I took her little baby into my arms and held her tight. She was just perfect, beautiful in every way, content, and asleep. I noticed her breathing and felt my rhythm sync with her own. I looked up to see the mother smiling down at me encouraging me to just hold her. We said nothing to one another. Everything that was important to communicate, we passed on in silence with only her sleeping baby between us. After a few more quiet minutes, I handed her back and they soon departed. I will never forget that young mother's face, the way her baby felt, and how they both made me feel. I will never forget.

The last *special moment* I will share occurred after my brother decided that it was time to let go. This *moment* involved two airline employees of JetBlue. It was so extraordinary that I decided to write a letter to the *head honcho* at JetBlue. I am sort of infamous for letter writing and decided that one was required.

I did deliberate, since this was post 9/11, and I wasn't sure how kosher it was to have been invited into the cockpit. But, under the circumstances, since we were boarding (I was almost last to board) and since I knew the CEO was himself a pilot, I took a flyer. Also, I was pretty sure that not many went out of their way to write a note telling of a positive airline experience. I thought he might find this to be a welcome departure. Here is my letter slightly edited from the original to correct for grammatical errors and repetitiveness (I am prone to both):

Mr. Dave Barger,

CEO

JetBlue

118-29 Queens Blvd.

Forest Hills, NY 11375

Dear Mr. Barger,

I would like to take some time to tell you about an extraordinary moment on an ordinary flight.

I have been a JetBlue traveler for many years, commuting
between Burbank (and now, LAX—thank you very much) and
NY, to see my twin brother who was severely disabled by a rare
neurological disease. After a nine-year-battle, he passed away.

Shortly after his passing, I went back to NY to spend time with
our ninety-year-old father. I was on my way home, after some
of the most difficult days of my fifty-one years. I was on flight
637 on January 20th. Right before boarding, I received a very
touching email from a co-worker and friend of my brother's.

My brother was very much on my mind as I boarded the plane.
As I entered, I looked into the cockpit. It was beautiful; a dazzling
array of technology and lights against a clear dark NY sky. My
brother's passion in life was flight. He flew fixed wing aircraft and
helicopters for years and years whenever he had the opportunity.
As I peered in awe into the cockpit, a woman inside invited me to
step in to take a better look. She had a warm smile. I thought she
was the flight attendant. As she, and a gentleman who I assumed
was the pilot, showed me around, I told them about my brother
and how he would have loved this moment.

That is when I became emotional and started to cry. The woman encouraged me to sit down in the pilot seat. I gingerly sat on the edge of the seat. She insisted that I sit properly in the seat to get the *feel* of command. This was her seat. She was the pilot. As I sat there, through my tears, I did what I knew my brother would have expected me to do: get it together, be strong and smile. She then asked if I had a camera and took my picture to record the moment. I only caught her first name on her nametag: Nancy. After she took the picture she gave me a hug and I took my seat.

If I can help it, I will never fly with another airline other than yours. I will never forget her and her act of generosity and kindness. We traveled through many storms that night. The flight was bumpy and yet, I had never felt so calm and secure with her in command.

I thought you should know.

My very best wishes for clear and calm skies,

X

Unlike Blanche who seemed trampled on by *strangers*, they have so often uplifted me. For all of those moments, to all of those people, I send my heartfelt gratitude.

LAMAZE IS FOR WHEN YOU TAKE YOUR KID TO CAMP OR COLLEGE

Birds have it easy: they fly around, pick a mate, build a nest, sit on a few eggs for awhile, the eggs hatch, they find a few worms, feed their chicks until they are ready to fly away and boom—everyone goes their separate ways. Simple.

Well, that's for the birds. No one ever told me how deep the attachment between parent and child would be. It's such a powerful love where the objective is to bring them up in order to let them go. When kids are little, you just assume they will be with you forever. Having your children leave you, while inevitable, is a very big abstraction.

This pending separation became very real when my little

daughter announced that she was ready to go away to summer camp. My big one never wanted to go to camp. She is such a good girl. My little one had other ideas, selfish little bitch. I couldn't believe she was out-growing *Camp Mommy*. What about all those fun road trips during the summer? How could anything beat the search for the biggest French fry in Idaho, playing with the Pilgrims at Plymouth Plantation, or the miles of trails hiked in the middle of really hot summer days? Yet, she wanted to be with kids *her own age* and at a sleep-away camp no less.

The mature rational part of me did see her point. I went to sleep-away camps throughout my early years. How could I deprive her of learning how to short-sheet beds, lock her evil camp director in her cabin and then pull the fire alarm, skinny dip under the stars, make campfires, and life-long friendships? I cannot let her go. I have to let her go.

I did let her go.

I thought I was handling it reasonably well. I filled my days with outdoor summer activities and pathetically hovered over my oldest daughter who seemed very busy living her own life. The two weeks felt like eight. The countdown to pick up my personal person from that awful place began.

The day before I planned to pick her up started out as a routine day. I popped in the car and headed for a walk at the beach. I noticed the gas tank was full. Halfway there, I got what I thought was a *fabulous* idea. Why don't I just go up now, spend the night at one of those cute little places right near camp and be the first in line to pick her up? I sometimes amaze myself with how smart I am. I banged a U (legal) and headed home to take some overnight stuff and maybe my camera in case I wanted to grab a few shots of the local scenery. Four hours later, I was almost there, and it was then that I decided that now might be a good time to share my most excellent idea with my family, especially my husband.

Me: "Hi, guess where I am?" He did not exactly sound like he was up for a guessing game so I immediately told him.

Husband: "Did you bother to see if you could get a hotel reservation?"

Me: "Not really, but no worries, there are a ton places in town."

Husband: "What's the name of the camp?"

Me: "Are you kidding me? Skylake, why?"

Husband: "Are you kidding me? Skylake **YOSEMITE** Camp, hello . . . the National park; one of the biggest summer destinations in the country, are you crazy? Once again . . ."

Then the call somehow dropped. I was sure it was just a bad cell connection. I turned up the radio and continued on my adventure, happy that soon I would be seeing my little chick.

I rolled into the last town before the park and only miles from camp. I passed a Starbucks and a couple of cute restaurants. Such a cute town; this works for me. I was already planning my restful evening and delightful morning as I passed several motels with neon signs reading, "No Vacancy." Hmm, maybe they just hadn't yet updated their signs. I decided to just stop and inquire.

By the time I had left my eighth motel, I was certain they were all on top of their room inventories. I became just a tad edgy after discovering that I had exhausted all the lodging possibilities in town. Ever the optimist, I left my name and cell phone number with each motel on the chance that a vacancy would appear. This place obviously needs more capacity. How could Trump, Hilton, Hyatt, Wynn, whoever, overlook such an attractive opportunity? I thought for sure someone would decide to leave town in the late afternoon on their summer vacation. And just then, the phone rang: jeez, my sixth sense sometimes scares even me. Wrong, it was my husband. I had two rings left to decide if I should answer it.

Husband: "Any luck or will you sleep in the woods with Yosemite Sam?"

Me: "As a matter of fact, Steve Wynn has opened up a new five-star hotel and offered me a complementary suite and a roll of quarters."

Husband: "So, no rooms."

Me: "No, but I'm first on the list for a room all around town; first, ahead of everybody else."

Husband: "I'm sure you are. Who else would be so stupid? If all else fails, go to camp. They might have somewhere you could bunk."

It was a short conversation. No way would I ever go to the camp and embarrass my daughter in front of all of her friends and counselors. I'd rather sleep in the car.

After the long drive and my motel scavenger hunt, I was hungry and needed a shot of tequila. After a yummy Mexican dinner, I noticed how dark it had become and how it was just a tad chillier. Did I bring a sweater? Oh well. Just as I was getting in the car, my phone rang. It was a motel in town letting me know that a room had just opened up and to give them fifteen minutes to clean it. My, they must have a big cleaning crew, fifteen minutes is fast. I was happy and relieved that my call came in; all was right in the universe.

My welcome refuge was an independent motel, not a part of any large chain. Good, I like boutique hotels and prefer the intimacy and service they provide. My, this *is* Spartan. I signed the papers, was given a metal key (charming, I haven't seen one of these in years), and then I was offered a paper bucket in case I wanted to go the motel next door to use their ice machine. The inn-keeper also let me know that the office would soon be closed until morning if I wanted to borrow a magazine or a Bible. I thanked her profusely and let her know that I was good without the ice and was comfortable with my Bible studies.

The room was . . . fine. I was pretty sure that hair in the sink was mine. I settled in, and after a while called home to share my good fortune. After watching the local news, it was time for bed. I was just starting to fall a sleep when I heard loud voices from the adjacent room. Then someone started banging on the door that separated our rooms. My heart jumped into my throat when they began to jiggle the door handle. If you can picture some dumb-ass mommy in a polka-dotted nightshirt clinging to the ceiling, that would be me. I was in the Bates Motel with psycho killers, or maybe even zombies, who were trying to break down the door and kill me. I jumped out of bed and frantically began to pile all the furniture I could move to the door that stood between oblivion and me. How would I get out of there alive? I called the office. No answer. I should have taken that Bible.

I didn't risk leaving the room, what if it was just a ploy to flush me out? The noise began to die down. Maybe the zombies were just a few dumb-ass drunks? I didn't want to call the cops and make a scene, and I was not going to call home. It was only six or so hours before the light of day; my plan was to make a mad dash for the car at dawn's early light. Six hours felt like thirty-six when dawn finally showed her face. I took a refreshing shower in 1.5 seconds and bolted into the car flooring it out of the parking lot and praying that no cops would see me. The fight or flight instinct began to dissipate only when that *house of horrors* became a spec in my rear view mirror.

My next great idea was to take a roadside nap, by a big lake near camp, since I had a few hours to kill (bad word), until I could arrive at Skylake. I was exhausted and quickly fell into a deep sleep, when suddenly I heard a tapping sound on my window. What is with all the sudden tapping and banging up here? It was a Park Ranger asking if everything was ok. And, by the way, "This was not a place to park." I circled the lake about forty times until the time when all were welcome at *Camp I Fucking Hate You*.

I was the first car in line to enter. There she was, my little angel, standing there like a beautiful oasis. As I approached her, she looked more like Pigpen; I couldn't wait to hug her. As I held her in my arms, everything that had just occurred over the last day simply faded away.

Daughter: "I missed you, Mommy."

Me: "I didn't even notice you were gone . . . I missed you too, sweetheart."

The summers that followed got mercifully easier and helped to prepare me for subsequent separations. My next great hurdle was sending my firstborn to college.

That day arrived overnight. There we were, unpacking her room in the freshmen dorm. My husband glared at me when I asked her if she had heard of the Peter Thiel Fellowship. What, the Fulbright is not the only game in town! When all was done, she seemed anxious for us to leave so that she could begin her great adventure. I surprised myself; I was the dry-eyed brave little toaster when it came time to say goodbye—a full day ahead of when we had planned to leave her.

What remained of our sad little family then went into our renegade's new hometown to explore and to meet some friends for dinner. It was a beautiful sunset that night and a great dinner. As we passed our co-ed's school on the way back to our hotel, I waved goodbye, proud of the big-little person that she had become . . . and then, the waves just came.

Damn.

I will just breathe. Who knew, Lamaze was time-released.

LEXUS SC400

My father and stepmother owned this car. I drove it whenever I was in NY visiting them, my brother, and the rest of the family. I had become very attached to this car. Everything about it made me feel secure, snug, and comfortable.

The car was sleek, perky, and fast. *She's a beauty* was a refrain I often heard, mostly from men at gas stations when I was filling *her* up. I thought it was interesting that men uniformly chose to feminize cars. *She* was a real head turner all right, and strangely, she attracted more attention as time passed. How cool, men look at aging cars just like they look at aging women. My little baby was becoming a classic: no scrap heap in her future.

There were times when she even caught the attention of New York's finest. Late one night when in NYC after having spent a great day with my kids and nephew, two officers pulled us over and very nicely suggested that I turn on my headlights and then they went on to provide directions to help get us get home, such gentlemen.

On occasion, inquisitive car lovers approached her, this amazing Lexus SC400, and me, to find out if she might be for sale. I always appreciated the compliments and overtures, but nothing doing. While she was not for sale at any price, only once, was I almost tempted by someone's offer:

I was again in NYC. It was a beautiful day and I was spending much of it in the car looking for a parking space. It is unbelievable how few parking garages exist near Columbia University. Then my luck changed. I turned a corner and noticed a spot adjacent to a fire station. I was immediately suspect and fearful that as soon as I were to park, a flair would shoot up to alert the nearest parking enforcement officer to come and either ticket me or have my car towed away. Nonetheless, I parked. I saw no sign or mark on the sidewalk to indicate that my little cherry (or me) would be in any jeopardy. To make absolutely certain of this, I thought I'd asked one of the nice firemen.

No sooner than having locked the door, two firemen approached me. Jeez, men in uniform really seemed attracted to this car. I didn't think they could ticket, tow or arrest. They seemed friendly. I asked about the space and was both happy and relieved to know that it was, in fact, a legal spot. Soon more of the fire people gathered around and we began a spirited conversation about her beauty and attributes.

One of the firemen was particularly enthusiastic, "I wanna buy this car." I explained that it was my dad's and that he would not want to sell it. "Let me talk to your daddy . . . I'll convince him, 'gimme his number." After a few minutes of continued banter, I began to realize that this guy was sort of flirting with me. This only became obvious to me when he said: "You come with the car, right?" Hmm, like my car, I must have looked shiny and polished. He walked away as I continued to chat with his co-workers, thanking them for complimenting my baby and asking them to please watch her in between fighting fires and rescuing cats from trees.

Then Mr. Flirty Fireman returned, and as he approached he tossed me a set of keys and with a big smile said, "Trade ya." The keys he so playfully tossed me were to the fire truck parked inside the station house. It was pretty cute. For a split second, I thought about it—it might be worth it just to see the look on my father's face as I pulled into his driveway with a NYC fire truck. Now that would be priceless. My next immediate thought was driving the fire truck on the Long Island Expressway. I wonder: can cops pull over a fire truck? I quickly snapped out of it, politely declined, and said my good-byes to my firemen friends.

Later that night when I returned, I saw my car, safe and sound. Wait—there was a paper on my windshield. My heart jumped. Thankfully it was a note and not a ticket: "If I ever changed my mind . . ." Cute. Let's just say, had the truck been a hook and ladder, I would have had a lot more trouble walking away.

Recently, my ninety-four-year-old dad thought it was time to pass the car on to a more active driver. It was sold in lightning speed with the proceeds going to a very good cause.

For twenty-three years she provided exemplary service and safely hauled around very precious cargo. For nine years she faithfully served me on my countless trips to NY. Every time I left my brother and I got into this car, I felt like it was giving me a hug.

Someone got a great car. I hope it was that fireman.

UP CLOSE

Cameras have taken me on so many adventures. I have owned many different cameras and lenses for them. They have conformed to times in my life when speed and agility were required, and when thought and patience were the demands of the day. I had a 35 mm when on the road, a 5x7 view-camera when not. One needs the right equipment at the right time. I became acutely aware of this under a big black tarp when setting up a shot with the 5X7 view camera in the middle of Manhattan. It, and I, attracted a lot of unwanted attention. I quickly returned to my 35mm. It was faster, safer, and much less conspicuous.

Now I have so much more time to play with my *old friends* and, like being with old friends, I continue to be reminded of why we remain close. The frame provides an elegant order, a way of seeing and making sense of everything around me. I see new things and see them in new and different ways, all courtesy of Mother Nature painting with light. Often, and in the stillness of the frame, you can hear your heartbeat. Everything comes alive and like hearing Richie Havens softly singing, *Follow* in your ear, you're not even sure if the moment is real. It's the sound of a shutter release that assures your grip in this world; it is both calming and exciting . . . and it does take one to many new places.

One lens has become my *go to* favorite. It is a one hundred millimeter macro lens. I love the intimacy of the macro world. It has shown me extraordinary things that had always been there, but had been completely unseen. I like shooting wide open with this lens, so that almost everything disappears leaving only the object of my interest in sharp focus. Often when you get this close, it's hard to hold steady. A slight tremor can alter what you see and can produce an unwanted and completely different image than what originally attracted you. This is why I now regularly use a tripod; it makes steady what your hand cannot. Even more, this magical lens allows me to gain distance and to see those same things with perspective, context, and clarity. It is a very versatile and powerful tool. I love the duality.

Early morning and twilight can produce mind-bending rich spectacular color and then, at other times, soft and tranquil light emerges. These are the most compelling and comforting parts of the day, like what waking up and going to sleep should be. Long exposures are often required to get the most from these parts of the day. I have taken many pictures under thirty seconds. Recently, I made one picture with a much longer exposure (over two minutes) and for that I had to carefully time the shutter's release. It did not turn out perfectly, but it did show me quite a lot. I will continue to try until I get it right, until I am able to get what I see.

Some day I may try and release the shutter to let the light in forever. I have no idea what that may produce but perhaps, it will be worth the time.

HUMPS OR BUMPS?

A street signpost in my neighborhood reads *bumps* yet; painted on the road the *bumps* are referred to as *humps*. These are the kind of things that rob me of my will to live. The same people responsible for parking signs that are often intentionally ambiguous must also be responsible for these signs. Former NYC Mayor Ed Koch said of NYC's parking signs, "You have to be a Talmudic scholar to understand all the parking rules." I should have paid more attention in Hebrew school. Really, is there any reason why they can't be made clear? A few suggested improvements: "Don't even fucking think about parking here," "You're not serious are you?" "Permit parking only, others scram." These I understand and can appreciate.

Likely we have all seen and fallen victim to these *other* signs. They are municipal dirty tricks designed to make you miserable each and every time you think, "Look, a spot—this is my lucky day."

My *Network* moment came in Santa Monica after receiving a ticket under one of these logic-defying signs. To add insult to injury, a man at the scene of the crime commented, "That must be the most profitable spot for the City of

171

Santa Monica. I wish I had a cut." The appeal instructions that came with my sixty-four dollar ticket *clearly* stated that I could submit a written explanation to contest the ticket. No ambiguity there.

I provided a thoughtful interpretation of the sign along with photos of the crime scene. The wheels of justice turn quickly when money is owed. Less than a week later, I received a letter from the City of Santa Monica letting me know that the summons needed to be paid *prior to* my having access to a judge. Hello City of Santa Monica: ever heard of *Due Process*? Parking and traffic court may be the only one in the land where you are presumed guilty and have to prove your innocence. I was determined to stand up for my rights and fight this injustice.

Dinner that night was spirited. I presented my case to my lawyer/husband and two children. It was more like mock (me) court: "Again? Can't you read, oh wait . . . I forgot . . . English is a second language." Harumph. I produced my evidence. "I want to initiate a class action lawsuit. I'm sure hundreds, thousands, hundreds of thousands of people, maybe more, have felt that their rights have been unjustly trampled upon. This is like organized crime; there could be RICO violations here." I was desperately trying to enlist support from my family. All I got was an eye roll from my youngest daughter, a look of contempt from my husband, and a request to buy more ketchup from my firstborn.

I turned to my trusted paralegal, Google, and quickly

learned about people who had successfully sued munici-
palities for ticketing cars that were parked at broken meters
(right on brothers and sisters). I was emboldened and did a
search to see if William Kunstler was still alive. How did I
miss that? RIP Bill. Others, with righteous indignation and
equally bad comb-overs, must have taken his place. I was
determined to find a legal champion to right the wrongs
that threaten our very way of life, liberty, and the pursuit
of parking.

A few days later, I was plotting my strategy when I received a summons for Jury duty. I felt this was a conspiracy
involving several government agencies to get me to alter
my course. There must be a mole at the ACLU.

I had been successful in avoiding jury duty in the past.
The last two times I had been called to serve, I had carefully
scheduled my start date around Jewish holidays knowing
that this would likely produce both atonement and post-
ponement. The child-care deferrals also seemed to work.
This time I was not given the option to defer; it was an
order to appear. Just as well. This could somehow be an
opportunity.

My day to find justice finally arrived. When I drove up,
I was happy to be given an *ok to park here ticket* and was
directed to a big structure adjacent to the courthouse. Nice
building, funny how all the signs seem pretty clear there.
The security guys were very nice and I was given an official
Jury Duty badge.

I went into a large room with many others and waited to

receive instructions. I noticed a woman in the office and went up to inquire when we might break so that I could talk to a judge in parking court. She was not certain that anyone in the building had that jurisdiction but she offered to make some inquiries.

I went and sat next to two young women, one who looked ready to give birth at any moment. Jeez, people will do anything to get out of jury duty. I began to think of all of the things I might be able to say to be disqualified if it looked to be a long and/or boring case. I once heard a story about a woman who claimed to believe only in Karma, I could probably get away with that, I have a few pictures somewhere on my iPhone taken in Bhutan with me and a few Buddhist monks. My concentration was broken only when a Jury worker came out to instruct us. She was a fine example of what one might hope for from a government employee: she was bright, efficient, and in possession of a sense of humor. This could be more entertaining than comedy traffic school.

Her most detailed instructions were how to productively spend our time while we waited, waited, and waited some more. She pointed us to a snack room and identified some of her favorite selections and then went on to list some of the magazines available to us in the lending library in the back of the room. Wow, cooperation between two government agencies, the library, and the court.

She then informed us that today would be different from all others. On this day, the court, and all those in the building, would be participating in *The Great Shake Out*, a statewide earthquake preparedness drill. Even more instructions were given; I was taking more notes than I ever did in college. When the alarm sounded, we were instructed to *duck and cover* for two minutes under our chairs—the ones that looked like they had been on loan from a local elementary school.

Afterward, when the instruction was given, we would line up, and in an orderly fashion, move down the stairs and out of the building. My, justice is so complicated. I was envisioning a conga line of lawyers, judges, clerks, murderers, bank robbers, bankers, bank robbing bankers, and parking violators dancing out of the building. This could be exciting, especially if anyone attempted to escape.

I occupied my time by trading baby and childcare stories with the mother to be. Then, the alarm rang. Oh, one more instruction, we were not to photograph in the building. Dang, this scene could have been a runaway YouTube hit. The room was filled with so many super-sized people all trying to stuff themselves under their tiny chairs. It was hilarious.

Then, as per our instructions, we lined up in a single-file to exit the building. I saw this as an opportunity to approach someone in a suit to see if I could find a constitutional lawyer, or anyone who looked the part, and who was willing to champion my cause. I didn't have much success.

Nonetheless, I was very impressed with the way the drill

was organized. Group leaders carried very big and clear signs identifying where every group should congregate. Our jury leader carried a sign that said, *Jury Members*. Other signs included: *Lying scumbags and their lawyers*, *Lying scumbag lawyers and their clients* (this was by far the largest group). Everything about the drill seemed very organized and clear. Whoever was responsible for having produced the signs for this event need to talk to their colleagues in the Parking-sign department!

By mid-afternoon, we were told that we were no longer needed and would be excused. We lined up (single-file) to get our certificate of service from our tour of duty. When it was my turn at the window, the entertaining jury duty instructor had, as promised, looked into my issue; no one at this courthouse would be able to hear my case, sorry. She then gave me instructions to the courthouse for parking violators.

Exhausted from my tiring day of instructions, I decided to grab some coffee before my drive home. I was standing in line (single-file) and began to chat with a bailiff who was on his break. I told him my parking injustice story. He was sympathetic and offered his wise counsel: "Next time take a bus."

TWO

I once mentioned to a friend my belief in a *life beyond* what we know or can see. For me, it seemed irrefutable, for on every corner in every town; there exists a Bed, Bath & *Beyond*. I've journeyed into many a store asking probing questions to the apostles of bedding about the *Beyond* section. While there, I would stop and wonder about the thread count in *Heaven* as I looked at all of those fluffy white pillows and comforters.

What follows is the eulogy I wrote and the Rabbi read at my brother's graveside memorial:

It will take much time to thoughtfully put into words who Michael was, and what his life meant.

This will be a start.

Mike was an original. He had a unique way of looking at the world and making sense of it.

He was an explorer and journeyman. He had an insatiable love of life and filled his with people and rich experiences. Michael was: insightful, wickedly funny, loved to meet new people, loved a party, loved a great story, loved to make people laugh, loved food and wine, loved music of all kinds, and loved the beauty of what he saw from

the many places he traveled. He cherished his friends and built many circles of *family* in places throughout the world. His great joy was in mixing it up and introducing friends to each other.

Michael had the mind of an engineer, the soul of an explorer, and the heart of a wise man, which he extended without hesitation to people he found in need. To many, he was known as *doc,* he knew how to fix things to make them right. Mostly, he did this for others. For Michael, his inner life presented much more of a challenge, one that I think he had time to resolve and find peace with during his last years.

His passion was to fly. He fell in love with flight when he was very young, in a small plane, in a clear sky somewhere over Toronto. I remember the look on his face when cousin Elmer gave him *the stick* for the very first time. By the time Mike was able to afford flight, he knew almost everything one could from books and manuals. He flew many types of aircraft in as many places as he could. He logged hundreds of hours. He never bothered to get his license . . . he always liked the company of others. After all, this was what he knew. He was a twin.

I am sending him off with several things that are very Mike: a few Cuban cigars, a shot of rum, pictures of his family, and a pilot's log which I found in his belongings last night. It was clean and blank. Fitting. Rather than his flight log filled with where he had been, he will fill this one with new experiences and adventures. I also found the first stuffed animals we had. They were twin squirrels. We had named them *Squeaky* and *Airmail*. I have no idea why we named the former, the latter was because we used to throw him at each other and yell "Air mail." At first I thought to give him *Airmail*. This morning, when I woke up, I realized that this was wrong. They have never been apart. It is fitting that they stay together and go ahead with Mike. Like those stuffed animals, we will never really be separated. In life I went first, as he always said, *to check it out*. In death, he will be the first to explore.

Above all, from this very tiny peek into a life, Michael was proud.

He took pride in what he did and in those he loved. He loved *his kids*: A & L and considered them his own. He loved the children of his dear friends. He was so proud to be an Uncle, to be a Godparent. He was proud to be a twin.

I was honored to be his.

MS. POTATO HEAD GETS A NEW NOSE

After having recently completed some major home improvements, I decided I would be next. I'm not sure who needs more maintenance, a (more than) fifty-year-old house or a (more than) fifty-year-old woman. At any rate, it was time to put myself in the *fix-it* shop. I had a few things on my list mostly from the neck up, but I was open to suggestions.

First priority was my nose. I couldn't breathe. I saw this as a metaphor. I had broken it sixteen years earlier when my then two-year-old daughter hurled her 8-ounce bottle filled with milk at me. She swore it was an accident. I've never liked milk. After this incident, I now had a badly deviated septum coupled with *age related* cartilage disintegration. My nose was barely functional. To add insult to injury, my nose traveled east to west from the middle of my face. Since the prizefighter look was not one I was going for, without a doubt, Ms. Potato Head would have to get a new nose. Check box #1.

Next on my list: my teeth, specifically my two front teeth.

Over the years, they began to overlap. Again, this was not a particularly good look. While the thought of adult braces wasn't terribly appealing, worse was the constant refrain I began to sing to myself: ". . . all I want by Christmas are my new front teeth." I had to get that stupid ditty out of my head. Check box #2.

It was late August to early September when I decided to check both boxes at the same time. I figured by December I'd be good to go. After all, I had been consulting with experts—kids with braces and young girls who recently had nose jobs. I had also planned a family trip to London over Christmas, so time was of the essence. Piece of cake, I could get this done, or so I thought.

I made an appointment with my ENT (Ear, Nose and Throat doctor) to move forward quickly. Imagine my surprise when my long-time ENT said, "You're going to need a plastic surgeon, I wouldn't touch this." "Oh great . . . and where am I going to find a plastic surgeon in LA?" I was trying my very best to charm him into changing his mind. "Hello, the *N* in ENT . . . did you miss that day in med school?"

He just ignored me and went on to explain how it would likely be a three-hour *procedure* with some grafting necessary. I didn't really stop to think deeply about the details he described. I was stuck on the word *procedure*. What exactly happened to the word *operation*? He gave me what seemed like two hundred names and started to outline the benefits of one over another. At the rate we were going, I didn't think I'd get out of his office by Christmas; let alone get the *operation* done in time. There were too many names to remember and they all sounded alike. Thankfully, I re-called that I had a distant relative by marriage that was a well-known and highly respected Plastic Surgeon in Santa Monica. I'd start there.

The plastic surgeon's office was very familiar—he shared it with my kid's dermatologist, also a well-known and high-ly regarded doctor. I too had been a patient. I went to see her years ago for a baseline full body scan. I remember it fondly: "You have a lot of nerve . . . I haven't had many people come in for a full body exam after having obviously been out nude sunbathing. Are you here for a lecture?" Note to self: don't do that again. I was happy to learn that all that time spent dipped in baby oil and tanning at high school and college did not produce a giant freckle or mass of mischief.

Back to the plastic surgeon:

Immediately following all the usual pleasantries, he quickly let me know that he would not be *the guy*. It would be an involved surgery (Note: he referred to it as *surgery*). It would be approximately three hours, and he suggested that it was better left to someone who specialized in reconstruc-tive rhinoplasty.

Reconstructive that was the first time I had heard that term applied to my procedure/operation/surgery. At any rate, I had known that this doctor was more of a *breast man* nonetheless; I thought it best to speak with him and figured he would have definite opinions as to who should make me a new nose. He gave me two names: both in Beverly Hills. As he was mentioning a city I did not care for, a city I loved popped to mind: Rome, as in, *when in.*

"Since I'm here . . ." I didn't even have to finish the sentence . . . when he said, "take your shirt and bra off, I'll be back in a couple of minutes." This was, after all, my time to explore various home improvements. He and his nurse walked back in, and he immediately began to speak into a tape recorder. As if I wasn't attached to the boobs he was inspecting, he began to describe them using terms I had never heard a man use when talking about breasts. "Are those fancy words and terms for lift and make bigger?" I asked. He intelligently ignored me and began to outline what he described as a simple augmentation.

Here's what really caught my attention, "Were you aware your left breast was ever so slightly lower than your right?" Everything from that moment on went dark; I began fixating on the notion of Asymmetry and my own. This revelation was guaranteed to drive me crazy. Now and forever more, I would look in the mirror and instead of seeing a small Rubens, a Picasso would be staring back at me.

How can this be? Balance and symmetry are so important to me. For sure, this would be my third box. Could I get it done before Christmas? If only I had kept my mouth shut and my shirt on. I spent the better part of that afternoon trying on and considering various boob sizes. All I really wanted to do was to go back to BC, Before Children.

The consultation ended with the doctor's business manager who let me know that he had generously extended a thirty percent reduction in fees for his services. A thirty percent reduction for about a thirty percent enhancement . . . ah: balance and symmetry—I would need to give this serious consideration.

I was still reeling from my last doctor visit as I sat in the waiting room of one of the nose docs recommended by the breast guy. His office looked like a Four Seasons, which worked for me at that moment, since I really wanted to order a drink. It was only 10:00 a.m. Ok, I could do a Bloody Mary—I was a little tense.

Every morning since the meeting with Dr. Tits, all I was able to see and think about was Picasso's Seated Woman (Marie-Therese). Damn, pull one thread . . . Ok, concentrate. "I'm here to talk to talk about my nose, breathing, Christmas."

The doctor quickly took command, a good trait in a surgeon. He briefly examined my nose and mentioned that it would likely be a three-hour procedure. I was happy for the consensus on the time required, but less so with his use of the word, *procedure*. I would be mature and look past it.

Just as I was beginning to relax, I noticed his hands. Damn, damn, damn . . . his hands. I have always had this thing with hands; blame it on Michelangelo and Sherwin Anderson. He had thin pointed fingers and he was wearing NAIL POLISH! In my twisted little brain this was a non-starter. This was not going to end with his hands in my pocketbook or up my nose. I quickly got out of there and went straight to the Four Seasons for a Bloody Mary.

I ended up being referred by yet another doctor to a head and neck Plastic Surgeon in Westwood with whom I felt immediate comfort. Mercifully, this doctor had good hands. He was around my age and we seemed simpatico in many ways: he felt that drinking too much before operating was not good, he too thought the word *procedure*, while *au courant*, was stupid and misleading, he greatly appreciated balance and symmetry and agreed that gray hair in LA would soon be a ticketed offense.

I kept my boob issue close to my vest, but I did share with him that I would soon be fitted for Invisaline braces. As it turns out, his wife had been thinking about Invisaline as well. I liked the way he talked about her, "She picked the right guy to keep her young." Indeed, she must be a smart girl, marrying a plastic surgeon, that's planning . . . I should have considered this. Next, he took pictures of my face and played on the computer drawing my new nose, which looked remarkably like my old nose before time, gravity, and my malicious two-year-old had their way with me. We spent quite some time spinning the wheel on many subjects from the serious to the seriously stupid. Clearly, he was going to be *the guy* to stick some silly putty up my nose and to engineer a permanent Breathe Right.

As an added bonus, my guy, *the guy*, had an equally colorful office manager. We just clicked. She understood the importance of having Christmas tea with the Queen and squeezed me in his busy schedule to help accommodate my travel plans. December 4th would be my day with infamy, leaving enough time to heal so I could get on that plane twenty days later.

She assured me, a couple weeks rest, a push broom of Bobbi Brown, and I'd be good to go. I signed a bunch of papers and took out my Amex card (it helped that he was thousands of dollars less than Dr. BH Shiny Nails). As I was leaving, my guy, *the guy*, came over for a few final words, all very reassuring. Somewhere in all our banter he used the word *harvest*. My only association with that word was with Neil Young. Cool. I left feeling like I was in exceptionally good hands.

Flash forward.

I woke up from surgery with Dr. Nose's face in mine. "I'm so sorry, I'm so sorry." WTF, did he have a little *oops* with the scalpel, did I still have a nose, a third nostril, what? It was more complicated than I thought, I needed to take my time, and the surgery took seven hours. WTF . . . did he say SEVEN HOURS? Was that with a lunch break? Seven hours, a heart transplant takes less time. Ok, maybe that's the median time, but still, seven hours! "Will this affect my recovery time?" "YES." He was very apologetic and sympathetic saying that my trip was definitely off the table since I was on his for twice the expected time, and then some.

I didn't feel any pain from my nose or face, but my head was killing me. My grafts were extensive, from the base of my ear covering several inches along the left side of my head. I now have a very different association with the word *harvest*. He soon left and in walked Nurse Ratched. I am not kidding—she was so mean and abrupt. I had barely gotten my blue bonnet off before she hustled me out of there. Then with an accusing tone she said, "That was a crazy-long surgery, how much cocaine did you do?" Coke? WTF, was I in Westwood or Nuremberg? What had I done in a past life to deserve her? Then came her warnings: "Follow all your post-op instructions, don't blow or touch your nose, and don't wear glasses for a year." What? I live in LA!

I was so happy to get home. I have no memory of how that actually happened.

The next month I spent under a rock, or more specifically, burrowed in my daughter's bedroom popping painkillers and rediscovering television shows, I mean, *content*. Like with the word *procedure*: I'm not sure what was wrong with the terms *programs or programming*. Was this renaming or re-appropriation of terms really necessary? I'm not averse to progress or change, just the opposite. It just needs to make sense and/or be additive. Another case in point: Asian vs. Oriental. I'm sorry but Oriental is so much more evocative: filled with mystery, romance, allure—*The Orient Express*? Did anyone change this to *The Asian Express*? The Orient Express inspired great authors and filmmakers, *The Asian Express* . . . what would that be, fast food? Oriental carpets, beautiful, majestic . . . try substituting *Asian*. Ok, maybe it's a little colonial.

I really have got to discontinue these painkillers.

Anyway, while I loved discovering Netflix and as brilliant as some of these shows were, this was a very challenging period of time in my life. I yearned for the days of just being preoccupied by my lopsided boobs. Instead, I looked like someone had taken a snow shovel to my face. Every few hours, I jumped out of bed to see, as if by magic, if my face had reappeared, and instead, all I got was this distorted reflection accompanied by a dialogue loop, *mirror, mirror on the wall, whose the dumbest bitch of all?* After all, I did this to myself. It was elective, sort of.

On my first post-op visit, I walked into a packed office filled with young girls all dreaming of a perfectly chiseled nose and the perfect life that inevitably awaited them. If you could see the look of horror on their faces when they saw mine, I felt like The Elephant Man. I kept saying to them, "It was massive reconstruction from a life long abuse of coke." I figured I might as well scare them straight. "Really, he's a great doctor, compassionate, believes in balance, symmetry." My new friend, sensing my discomfort and not wanting to lose business, scooped me up and took me by the hand into a small side office away from the horrid stares.

In walked my guy. Not only was Christmas off the table, but the timetable of total recovery where all of the swelling would be gone and when I would see *the final result* would be more like eighteen months; not six months to a year. He was confident, happy with his work, and felt that I would have a perfect outcome: functionally and cosmetically. I totally trusted him. I did turn out to be *a slow and stubborn healer*, no surprise to anyone who knew me. That was Box #1.

As for Box #2, Invisalign works, but they are hardly invisible. Orthodontists don't tell you about these little stubs they need to weld to your teeth; that make it really easy for green shit to hang off of them. So yet again, I did not sport a very attractive look. Theoretically, checking both boxes at once made sense . . . theoretically. After a few months, I found myself whimpering in the orthodontist chair pleading with him to: "Take these fucking things off." I thought my teeth looked straight enough.

Against his better judgment, he agreed to remove them; I'm sure he just wanted me out of there. Within a couple of months, I returned to show him how my teeth were once again on the move. In all the years of practice, he had never agreed to take anyone's braces off prematurely. I would have to get them on again for another few months. He didn't charge me, saying that it was his mistake and he would never again succumb to pathetic groveling. I appreciated this, and promised there would be no more crying in *big girl land*—so much for my timetable.

It's been almost a year. We had tea in London over the summer: Christmas in July. It was a good trip.

I recently bumped into *my guy* with his wife months later at a local farmers market. Her warm smile shimmered with her new Invisalign braces. As if by reflex, my doctor immediately started to touch and examine my nose in the middle of the crowded market. I turned to his wife, "Aren't you glad he doesn't do tits?"

Would I do it all again? I wouldn't want to, but . . . yes I would. I can breathe, my nose is straight, my teeth are straight . . . my head? Well, that's a work in progress. And as for Box #3, now, after showering and looking in a mirror, I just tilt my head ever so slightly and it all seems ok.

Long live the Queen!

X KA' MOES, OR PEOPLE I'VE RUBBED NOSES WITH

Early in my freshman year of college, I began an exchange of notes from an unknown admirer in the classified section of our school newspaper. He began this exchange with something like, "X (me) from Richmond (my dorm), I want to explore and reach new worlds with you," signed C. Columbus. My response, "Hi Chris, loose lips sink ships." This light-hearted banter went on for several weeks and was very amusing. Finally he asked to meet. On my way to the designated spot on campus, I stopped. The fantasy was so good, why trade it for anything real? I turned around and went elsewhere to meet some friends. I never heard from him again.

I'm not sure why, but I have always had more than my fair share of attention from the male species. In my experience, archetypes abounded. No matter how seemingly evolved, educated, and creative, most of the men attracted to me were a tad Neanderthal-like, and invariably wanted to club me over the head, drag me into their man-cave, to have me revolve only around them. I did find myself in a cave every now and again, but luckily I saw the writing on the wall. While walking with the beasts in the land of fire and ice could be fun, this type of relationship was always self-limiting. Perhaps if I had more of an interest in paleontology, it would have held more appeal.

I am grateful, however, for all those who came into my life and for the time spent together. I hope *some* of my past loves share the sentiment. It's a safe bet that most of my X's would never read this. Simply, it's not about them. I have only one, maybe two, regrets. I regret not having been more sensitive in saying good-bye to some, and I wish I could take a mulligan with one boy I went out with during college in upstate NY. If I could ever say I'm sorry, I would in a heartbeat.

The Eskimo language has thirty-two words for love, all with many nuances. It can be confusing.

Maybe rubbing noses *is* all that's really necessary.

Stay warm.

LIFE IN 1/80TH
OF A SECOND

Ah, photography: my love. Picture taking has led to many magical moments, some lasting only a fraction of a second and some with much longer exposures.

My high school boyfriend introduced me to photography. Imagine my surprise, when in my first college photo class, I realized that *making out was not* a requirement for developing film or printing pictures. At any rate, the hobby proved to be lifelong, the boyfriend was not.

Flash forward thirty-five years to a photo workshop in LA taught by a world-class professional photographer with many talented photographers attending . . . and me. At its conclusion, I decided to take the advice given by the instructor, "Take your work more seriously, don't be lazy, use a tripod, and slow down." While I was unsure about taking myself seriously, I did make a commitment to up my technical skills and to begin to use my bazillion dollars worth of digital camera gear, which I had neglected in favor of my iPhone camera. As soon as my *little one* was back in school, I would go on a trip to advance this mission.

I decided that I would Thoreau myself into nature for inspiration. Hiking in the woods with forty pounds of camera equipment just made sense to me. New England during fall foliage season was now on my radar. As luck would have it, friends offered their lovely ski condo in Dover, VT. This is where I dropped the pin on Google maps.

I had originally planned to take this trip solo since pulling over to the side of the road every five minutes to snap a picture or setting up a tripod under a waterfall in the middle of Bambi-land was not everyone's idea of a good time. None of my friends or family seemed terribly in favor of this even though I reminded them of my three or four badges earned while in the Girl Scouts. Two of my very best friends who knew how bad I actually looked in green and how undistinguished my time in Girl Scouts really was, offered to join me.

The Maple Syrup State did not disappoint. I did however need time to acclimate. There were so few cars, and such friendly people. Seeing someone wave from a car was not the hand gesture I had come to know while driving in LA. Every encounter with the locals in shops, taverns, artist studios, diners, or on hiking trails, was delightful. I also noticed that camera people seemed to easily find other camera people. I wonder how they know?

On one such occurrence we stopped, at the very end of a long day, to *take one last shot* of a beautiful marble quarry we had spied on our way to have dinner. It had great reflections in the pond that lived in front of it. I had to move quickly. I was losing the light and feared my friends would drive off without me. Out of nowhere a guy with a fancy camera emerged. I quickly learned his gear preferences, that he was from NYC, loved VT, and was on assignment for some magazine. Then he asked, who I was shooting for. I guess I must have looked the part: "The Sanity Times." It took him a moment, but he did laugh. I wasn't trying to be rude, but I was now conscious of my best friend standing beside me looking like she was about to hit me. He gave me his card and I quickly took a few shots.

The following day, while on the road to nowhere in particular, I remembered a not so great photo experience that I haven't recounted in many, many years. I was about nineteen when a relative asked me to photograph an important family event, a Bat Mitzvah. I had previously taken some informal family pictures for them, all of which turned out well. While I had done a lot of photography assignments, some professionally, this was to be the first *event* that I had been asked to shoot. Everything was going well until a very dear person to me, who was dying of cancer, showed up with her son. Even though I had recently seen her, her health status shocked and upset me. I had a drink, or maybe two.

Here's a good rule of thumb for a working photographer: don't drink at the event you are covering. My pictures (outdoor) got progressively fuzzier. The dinner was an indoor event requiring flash. No problem, I had a very professional unit. Only one problem, it did not properly sync to my camera that night. This was (and is) a very big problem. Imagine my surprise and horror when I picked up the dozen rolls of film I had shot and saw nothing, absolutely nothing. It was a very low moment. I vowed to never again, no matter what, **ever** photograph *a once in a lifetime event*. Theoretically this could have precluded weddings, but I threw that into the promise pile as well. Some people have recurring school/test nightmares; this was mine, or one of them.

Ok, that was then; this is now. We were having a good time ambling about the back roads of VT. We had planned to go to Woodstock, but at the rate we were traveling, we would more likely be eating breakfast there than a late dinner. We decided to travel instead to the little town of Weston.

We cranked the radio up and eventually rolled into Weston, a charming and picturesque place, driving about a half a mile past the main drag just to get the lay of the land. My friend pulled over so I could walk back into the town center and meet her there.

I was moseying down the street minding my own business when a car pulled up beside me. With two cameras dangling from my neck and a tripod over my shoulder, they couldn't possibly think I was the best person to ask for directions.

The couple inside did not look like they were lost or out

for a nice afternoon drive. She was in a formal gown and was holding a beautiful fall bouquet, and he was wearing his Sunday best. "We're getting married in the town square, can you be our photographer?" I stood frozen in silence and complete amazement. They must have thought they had stopped a non-English speaking person instead of just a barely able to speak English person. After what seemed like an eternity, these words effortlessly tumbled out, "Um, maybe, um, don't know, sure, maybe." She still had a smile on her face, but he looked as if he made a big mistake when he stopped me. I recovered, "I'll meet you in town, I want to walk." They politely agreed and drove off.

As I continued my walk, my pinball brain went into high gear. "What? What is the universe trying to tell me? Was this some new reality show, Karmic Camera? Just because they wanted to take their vows didn't mean I had to break mine. Where was that professional photographer from NYC that I met yesterday? Where was a busload of Japanese tourists when you need them? Maybe I could talk them out of the whole marriage thing; did they know all the divorce statistics? Then I thought, just walk, and shut the hell up.

As I came into town center, I saw them inside a gazebo with some official looking guy in a suit holding a big black book. They were slowly walking away. Jeez, that was fast; they must have cut right to the *I do's*. I started to run. The cameras were banging into me as if to remind me of my *I don'ts*. I began to shout, "Wait, wait, hold on . . ." I felt a little like Dustin Hoffman. It was quite the scene as people turned to see what all the commotion was about. This was very un-characteristic of me; not that I don't create commotion from time to time, but generally it's not loud.

"Hi, I'm happy to do this for you," I said. The groom extended his hand and introduced himself—Ok, while I'm breaking vows; I'm going to violate the privacy one. The bride said, "My name is Alexandra, but everyone calls me Alex," which just happens to be my daughter's given and nickname. I got very choked up. The groom was giving me that quizzical look again. I immediately began fumbling for my iPhone to show the bride pictures of my Alex while rambling, "I don't know what it is about weddings, they always seem to make me teary-eyed, does this happen to you?" Her makeup looked just fine.

Then, to work I went. I began carefully composing shots and checking and rechecking my settings. My photo teacher appeared in my mind's eye: "Slow down, don't be lazy, use a tripod if needed." The light was beautiful. Although I wanted to move them to a more scenic location away from people and cars, this was the spot where they married. They had been together for six years and had traveled to VT on a few days holiday, when they decided that this was the perfect time for them to be married. The rings, the dress, the suit were all purchased the day before. With each shot I became more and more relaxed.

The best shot was found in between shots. I had posed them for a few pictures and was just looking in my viewfinder for the next group of shots, when I saw her looking up at him as he pulled her closer. It was such a loving and intimate moment, and it was preserved for all time in 1/80th of a second.

I took a few more pictures and then wrote down his email address. The groom then told us that they were to soon be *shipped out*. He kept saying, "I wish there was something I could do for you," to which I responded, "You have no idea . . ." We said our good-byes. I shook his hand and hugged her tight silently wishing them a good life together.

Then I sat down on a park bench with my best friend by my side and ate fudge. She had bought four different kinds. You almost had to be alone to eat the peanut butter and chocolate.

It was a magical moment among several within a great week. I went home and quickly sent out the photos to the email address hoping I got that right. Two days later this was in my inbox:

Wow!!

I cannot thank you enough for all your help and photo taking.

You did such an amazing job.

One of the photos that you took we printed and framed for our mothers. This was our way of surprising them with the news of our wedding success.

Thank you so much for all your help, your grace, and your care to help a couple of people get married.

May the universe guide you unto your next photo opportunity.

Take care.

With Love,

"X"

You just can't do much better than that.

GOLF BY ASSASSIN

I played some golf in high school but not since then. I was a bit rusty. Over the past few years, I began to see the allure of golf courses—they looked so inviting. I thought perhaps golf could be a new and pleasant activity. While I was a little iffy about some of the clothes worn, golf had many appealing features: scenic walks, fresh air, the pace was right, it could be both social and solitary, and . . . it seemed peaceful.

I thought about a trip to Scotland to explore the Hebrides, a bunch of islands off its coast. National Geographic described these islands as "being at the end of the world." Since I'd spent so much time in my youth thinking about the beginning of the world, I felt I needed to see what the end looked like . . . and while I was there, those golf courses looked pretty darn nice. I thought I would just need to take a few lessons, so I wouldn't tear up all those finely manicured greens or generally be a menace to everyone else on the courses.

There are many places to play in LA, and over the years I received invitations to several private clubs. Since I was not a private club person per se, I started to look for public courses where I could take a few lessons and where I wasn't likely to see anyone I knew. I liked the thought of public being private. I found the perfect place, wrote down the number, and tucked it away. Now I just needed to find an accomplice to join me.

Before long, a good friend became my new golf pal and we were off to take our first lesson with a PGA Golf Pro. We liked him immediately. He had an easy style and an easy smile. He began our lesson by telling us a little about himself. He was a Vietnam vet, a highly trained rifleman, was on the pro circuit, was a single father who raised two highly accomplished daughters, and . . . he loved teaching golf. How interesting, what a cool background, this is going to be so much fun!

He went on to say that he spent some time in the Middle East. My friend is Iranian, and as we bantered about the good old days with the Shah, he went on to say that he worked nearby as an *independent contractor* in which he applied the skills he had acquired during his time in the military.

Fascinating . . . then I got distracted trying to think of the name of the actor who starred in *The Rifleman*. Thank G-d for Google; I now divide my life by BG and AG: before and after Google. Chuck Connors was *The Rifleman*. Not knowing would have bugged the crap out of me for the duration of the session.

Getting back to our lesson, he explained the geometry and physics required to successfully master the game. Geez, I like this guy. "Golf is simple. It's all about straight lines and angles." As he slowly demonstrated, I did take note of some of the expressions he used: *line of sight*, *targets*, and *taking your shot*. All sorts of things were buzzing through my head as I tried to absorb all this new information on the technique and philosophy of the game.

Our time went by faster than a speeding bullet. He showed us how to hold the stick and the location of the head and toe. We were very happy and proud of ourselves when we made contact with the ball. Before long we said our goodbyes and I made arrangements for our next lesson. He gave us each a *club* (I am such a fast learner), so that we could practice at home; it was so nice of him.

Feeling great, I started the car, waved my final goodbye until next week, and we drove off. When we were a block or so away, my friend started screaming, "What, are you crazy? You want to take golf lessons from an assassin?" "Former, former . . . possible assassin . . . what? He seemed very nice, and besides, everybody's got a past." We started to debate. My friend is a public defender and has a keenly developed instinct about people. I told her about the time I spent with a *former* Mossad agent trying, unsuccessfully, to get the film rights to a book he was writing, and how I once briefly dated a guy in the CIA. By the time I dropped her off, we were both laughing having determined that he was a man of good character, a fine teacher, and that she'd see me next week.

She was a last minute no-show the following Saturday morning. I was going in alone.

I met my assassin-turned-golf-pro-turned-instructor at the VA golf course, and we immediately got to work. I looked around happy to see that there were witnesses present, I mean other people playing. He kept saying, "You know, you have to relax," and, after a while, I did. I listened and watched intently. "I'm going to teach you how to play this game the right way. Over time the stroke should be easy. I love seeing the women play; they know how to get power from proper form using an easy and gentle swing. The guys are out just trying to kill it (I did note the word choice)."

Having said that, everything he taught made sense to me, I just needed to apply it. I repeatedly made contact with the ball most of the time, but I didn't have *the feel*. He was very patient, and like every good teacher, he showed me and told me things in multiple ways until I began to understand, to correct my form and more naturally integrate it into my swing.

I loved to watch him demonstrate. He had an effortless beautiful form. It was a nice day, and I was very happy to be there. Then, like a shot from out of nowhere he said to me, "You have a problem with trust, don't you?" **Bang**, a direct hit. Jeez, this guy was good: I just wanted to learn how to play golf.

Did we need to dig up Dr. Freud in the middle of the VA golf course? "Um, why do you ask?" I responded nonchalantly. "Here's what I want you to do, start your swing slowly." I followed his instructions, and then just at the top (the big L), he shouted, "Close your eyes and swing!" I followed his order, closed my eyes, swung down and BOOM I hit the ball. "Lets do it again, and a few more times." I took the next few swings with my eyes closed and made contact with the ball each and every time. It felt right, very natural, and relaxed. He seemed pleased. "That's enough for this week, see you next week. Practice your swing." We said our good-byes. As I watched him walk away, I thought, "Yeah maybe that's it . . . just close your eyes and take a swing." I'll keep that in mind. I'm going to like learning how to play this game.

An update: I've now taken three lessons. The assassin doesn't like using names; he uses numbers. It's a hold over from 'Nam. I'm now *Sixteen*. I'll take that. I refer to him in my emails to my golf accomplice only as *The Assassin*. I'm hoping the NSA understands we are just teasing about a golf instructor; especially one who I just today learned is a pacifist:

When he referenced a patchy area on the course as being the handiwork of a few mischievous gophers, I mentioned that I too have that same problem (in my backyard). I had recently gone to one of those do-it-yourself home improvement stores and asked the guy at the garden center for some *gopher be gone*, or whatever. He handed me something that was a poison; I said be gone, not be dead. I left empty handed.

The Assassin told me that he would never kill a thing, not even a bug; somehow I knew that. He suggested using cayenne pepper, so I bought some. While I'm at it, I have a recipe for smoky beef and bacon chili. Perfect, *pepper* two birds with one stone and hope for a *birdie*.

MOMMY JAIL . . .
IT'S A BLESSING

Mommy Jail is where a *jury of my mommy peers* sends me after they determine I committed *crimes* against my kids and some of their friends. I consider my time in *jail* to be well spent. Over the years scores of kids who have run through my house have all known where the candy drawer was located. Many times, these words have fallen out of my mouth as they stuffed theirs, "Remember, this is between us." Sure, many mothers were militant about sugar consumption, and I too believe in promoting healthy habits, but I just don't look that good in fatigues. Personally I prefer the color orange and my own style of parenting.

One night, as I lay in bed with my very big little fifteen-year-old daughter, free-floating memories of her as a baby danced through my head. My musings seemed to have limited appeal. Not wanting to be hurtful but also not wanting me to continue, she picked up her phone so that she could gently suggest that the time had come for her to do something else, and for me to get the hell out of her room. But the night was young; lets have some fun. Clearly, it was time for me to deploy another tactic:

Me: "Someday you will be me saying the same type of things to your little one, and by the way, just so that you know . . . anytime a baby is born, it's a blessing, anytime . . . although, I guess it's probably not a good idea to promote teen pregnancy."

She: "Mom! Now that comment would definitely get you a life sentence in your *Mommy Jail*."

Me: "Oh, come on, high school and college are so overrated, just think about it . . . if you start now, you'll have your very own yellow school bus full of tiny tots by the time you're forty. Hey, wait a minute, I could be the bus driver!"

She: "Sounds great, I could get my own reality show on TLC, *Twenty-One Kids and Counting*—and BTW, I love you mommy but no way are you ever driving my kids around."

Me: "You may have a point about the driving, but back to the subject at hand. You'd be years free from all those pesky period cramps . . . but . . . morning sickness is a bummer, especially with those horse pill vitamins they give you . . . I couldn't take them, they made me too sick."

She: "***What?*** You didn't take them?"

Me: "No, why? Are you missing anything?"

She held up both hands hiding her thumbs.

Me: "Good, you'll never hitch hike."

It went on from there. We laughed our asses off thinking about the possible names for her kids. By then: naming kids after cities (Phoenix and Paris) will be passé, planets will be all the rage (Pluto and Uranus). We were being very mature. Next, I found myself searching YouTube for the Monty Python clip where, in The Meaning of Life a woman drops her eightieth baby while working in a field, and says to her co-worker, "Could you pick that up, please?" I'm always so happy when I am able to broaden her horizons. She loved the clip and loved our playful time together even more.

Not wanting our time to end I began to tell her about the few times that I picked her sister up, in the second and third grade, during the middle of her school day, so I could take her for long drives up the coast. The school administrator was none too pleased as I signed her out and wrote, "just because," on the explanation line of the sign out paper. I didn't want to lie.

On one of those excursions as we drove up the coast, I spotted a large farm and decided to stop. We watched as many hard working men and women bent over to harvest what she just effortlessly reached for at the local grocery store. We had a long conversation imagining what their lives were like. We talked about food production, distribution, nutrition, what our favorite berries were, and the many ways they could be made into dessert.

On another day of playing hooky, we drove many miles to a favorite state beach I would occasionally frequent. We stood at the water's edge; hypnotized by the waves coming in and going out. Like the waves, we talked about the things one could count on but never really count. We talked about family, friends, and the concept of infinite love. With my arms around my little girl looking past the top of her curly head to the ocean as vast as the love I held for her, from out of nowhere a school of dolphins emerged. They triumphantly shot out of, and back into, the water in perfect 180° angles. We silently watched in amazement as they danced and played before us.

When it started to get a bit chilly, we got back in the car. I put *Let It Be* on the CD player as I pulled onto the highway with the top down and the heat up. After a few minutes drive I looked over and saw that she had fallen asleep. As we continued, I thought about the term *Joy Ride*, and in that moment, I fully understood its meaning.

We both cherished those mid-day rides.

There were many, many times where it became obvious that I held different views of what and how to parent: to each his own. Only once did the possibility of having to do **real** jail time cross my mind:

My little daughter has a friend who she has known since they were two years old. Her friend is an only child. They attend different schools. Her parents often travel and, because of the work that the father does, they receive many invitations to events and places that are quite unique.

One such invitation was extended to my daughter. They were invited to take the maiden voyage of a luxury ocean liner that would travel from Italy to Spain over several days. Only a hundred or so people (adults) would accompany the new crew. Taking this trip would require that my daughter miss four days of school adjacent to a planned school holiday.

That was the foreground, this is the background: this little girl was struggling socially in school. In many ways she is an out of the ordinary little girl which often segregates people like her from well, more ordinary kids. Generally, it was a time in her life when this little girl needed to feel the love and support of a true friend.

This was my daughter's concern when we discussed her going on this trip: she wanted to help her friend feel comfortable and not alone. To think that a luxury European cruise to a ten-year-old means what it might to an adult is either antithetical, or just stupid. My daughter's reason for going was exactly the reason why I wanted her to go.

Done deal in my mind, and happily my husband concurred. I let the friend's parents know of our decision, took both the kids out for ice cream, and stopped at the local bookstore to pick up a copy of <u>Treasure Island</u> for them to pass back and forth reading aloud during their adventure together. My kid also asked that I buy her Dramamine because, unlike her mother, she always felt sick on boats.

I wrote a note to her sixth grade teacher letting her know about this adventure and of my decision. It was not warmly received. She sent back a terse reply, and then began to make her disapproval known to my daughter. More backstory: my kid is a quick study, highly responsible, and disciplined (well at least I don't get sick on boats). She asked for the assignments that she would be missing and promised to do all of her homework to cover her absence prior to her leaving.

Still, snide comments to my kid continued from this disapproving teacher. This upset my daughter because she liked and respected her teacher. For that reason, I bit my tongue and just explained the importance of differing opinions in all facets of life and in learning. As far as I was concerned, the case was closed.

A week or so before the trip, the comments from her teacher became more frequent and culminated in this oh so unforgettable warning, "We will be having a test on the day you get back, I don't care how tired you are, you cannot miss it, and you better be prepared." She came home in tears. This is when I seriously thought about ripping her teacher's fucking lungs out. Like with Jimmy Carter and lust, it was just a thought.

I had not shared the details of what this other little girl was going through with this *teacher*. Simply, it was none of her business. That night, I wanted to teach my daughter a new word: *sadistic*, but I figured she would learn it at some point, hopefully, much later in life. I spoke with another teacher at her school who I liked and respected. Her mommy obviously took vitamins; she gave the trip two thumbs up.

The girls went on their trip and saw and experienced a

great many things. Both will always remember the week they spent together traveling through small towns on twisty narrow Italian roads being warmly greeted by the many people they encountered. They will remember exploring the ship, reading the story, and making up their own; as they traveled the high seas . . . and they will have pictures of them together both smiling with their arms around each other. I cannot think of a better way for them to have spent that time.

So, put me in mommy jail. My only requests are that I have an Internet connection, hot showers in the morning, my iPhone, and ok, maybe a bottle of vodka. Wait, one other request; it is that someday my girls spend a little time in mommy jail for committing the exact same crimes. I want to be certain that my grandchildren don't miss these little life lessons.

Ah, grandbabies . . . they're a blessing.

BLOOD, WATER, & THE LATE SHOW WITH DAVID LETTERMAN

Every now and then I'd find myself discussing *family*, or the notion of family, with my two daughters who noticed that they lived three thousand miles away from grandparents, aunts, uncles, and many, many cousins. I'd respond to their quizzical looks by saying things like: "Life just unfolded in this way, look another beautiful sunny day in LA, isn't it fun to travel on planes?"

As they matured (they) the conversation became more interesting. What does *family* mean? I pointed out that a family originates from the union of two people who were once strangers, or as I referred to it: a water and water cocktail (ok, maybe this involves some vodka). Is family then only blood related?

Both my husband and I have strong bonds with friends that are decades long, I refer to them as *lifers*. I count these people as *family* and define family as people who are with you no matter what. Nowhere was this more apparent than during the nine long years of my brother's illness.

Mike had a great friend from childhood. His name is also Mike. The *other Mike* and his family traveled great distances to visit *our Mike* several times each year. So too, did many of his other friends from college, work, his travels, and from his *fly-boy* circle of friends. He had so many incredible friendships.

Mike never married but had several long-term relationships. During a time where many *significant others* would have looked for the exit, his last girlfriend came back into his life **after** he became ill. She was there throughout much of his long illness to hold his hand and provide comfort to him. When I look down at the invisible medallion I imagine around my neck, the one where saints are lovingly displayed, I see her face.

Mike had many caregivers that also became his family. They lovingly circled around him in hospitals and long-term care facilities and made him feel at home.

Mike worked for most of his career at CBS, his last ten years on The Late Show with David Letterman. So many from his *Letterman family* came to see him and sent cards and letters throughout his illness. Dave once said about him, "I don't exactly know what he does, but he'll always have a job here."

When he was disabled but still living at home, they sent a car to pick him up so that he wouldn't miss the annual group shot of the show's staff. Every Christmas, without exception, Mike received the holiday gift that the show gave to its production staff. When I was raising money for biomedical research, they, along with so many of his friends from all parts of his life, generously made contributions. When Mike passed, it was his *Letterman family* who built a Facebook page for all to pay tribute.

Several people from the show kept in touch with me and recently, I received an email that stunned me: almost apologetically it said, "We kept his locker with all of his stuff still in it. Regrettably, we now need it. I'll send you his belongings." For all of those years, the Letterman gang kept more than just his locker; they, along with so many others, kept him going.

That's family.

And the good thing for me, now, we are all related.

Thanksgiving: next year at my house?

IF ONLY MY VIBRATOR WERE A MAGIC WAND

It may not be good to judge a short story by its title.

But, while we're on the subject of titles (and books) that did seem to satisfy expectations:

When I first heard the title, *Fifty Shades of Grey*, I thought, "Great, a book about photography, Ansel Adams, and the Zone System no doubt . . . oh, that zone."

I did read *Fifty Shades of Grey*. After all, in a former life it was essential that I kept abreast with popular culture especially with material that exploded to the upside. Aside from all the whips, chains, and cutlery, I thought the book's mass appeal laid in the fantasy of a woman being able to change a man, and in his allowing her to drive his fancy sports car without going nuts when something went asunder.

Back to the magic wand: there is some risk here of sounding like a wayward beauty pageant contestant. Were I to possess that magic wand I would wave it in such a way that hunger and thirst would be words only used in the context of desire for knowledge. Next, I'd create an international stamp with Rodney King's image on it. Then, I'd put more women in charge.

What would you do with it?
Post on FB: (I. Leigh Private) or @ileighprivate.com (try and keep it somewhat clean).

IS THAT YOUR FINAL ANSWER?

I still had some dirt under my fingernails the day after I buried my brother.

As I did when we were kids, I promised to tuck him in when his time to rest came. In my mind this meant filling in his grave myself, which I did with the help of my husband. When it was almost complete, my husband left, so I could finish the task. I wanted it to end as it had started, just the two of us. I was wearing a tee shirt with his favorite character on it, *Top Cat*. So many emotions, people, and scenes filled my mind as I filled that hole.

Even when things seemed dark, my brother and I found a way to lighten the mood and to mine the humor in the moment. When he was still living in his little house during the first few months of his illness, I was living with him as we made our *rounds* together visiting various medical experts. While he was resting upstairs, I was downstairs cleaning his oven, silently cursing him. He was such a slob. Suddenly, I heard a huge thumping/banging. It sounded like he had lost his balance and had fallen down the flight of stairs. I was so scared as I ran around the corner only to find him at the top of the steps laughing his ass off . . . you know those huge blue plastic Sparkletts water containers?

A few months later, a leading ophthalmologist had been examining him along with about eight others, presumably interns and residents. This seemed like a big treat for everyone as they lined up to peer into the microscope and into the mystery that my brother's case presented. The lead doctor called each person by name to have a turn looking into my brother's eyes, "Dr. X, Dr. Y, please take a look . . ." After the last name was called, my brother called my name. His timing was perfect. I went over and took a look, "Funky . . . is that a bird?" We thought this was pretty funny. A few others nervously laughed as well.

More time passed. He drifted in and out of consciousness in a hospital ICU for weeks with multiple issues and infections that most felt he would not be able to overcome. One of the nurses there thought she was providing comfort and counsel to me by offering this commentary, among other pearls of wisdom: "We're born alone, and we'll die alone." She was irritating. The second time she said this to me, I responded by saying, "Hello, I'm a twin . . . when I go I'm taking someone with me," and since she so loved insipid platitudes, I thought, I'd follow with one of my own, "And . . . no time like the present." She quickly left, never to be seen (by me) again. I can't be sure, but I thought I saw my brother smile. That was seven years before the dirt under my fingernails.

I was with my best friend, a day after I buried him, at his favorite bar/restaurant when visiting LA, Chez Jay. He loved the place and had mentioned its owner, Jay on several occasions. They had hot air ballooning in common. For some reason, I just wanted to be there that day to try and outrun my grief.

After several of whatever I was drinking, I got up to go to the restroom. I was standing outside the bathroom door waiting my turn, and when I looked up, I noticed a hand-painted sign on the side of the wall, "All You Need is . . . (two red hearts)." It took my breath away. In all of the fine museums our mother had taken us to throughout our childhood, in all of the art galleries I have been to, art books I have looked at, artist studios I had visited, I had never seen any work of art as powerful as what I was now standing before. I took a picture of it with my iPhone, wiped away a few tears, and went back to rejoin my friend feeling as if I was meant to see that image.

In the two years since I photographed that picture, I've often thought about its impact in that moment. I had not been back to Chez Jay since and decided it was time to go back to once again behold this *masterpiece*. I also wanted to take another photo, this time with my big camera. I went back and discovered, to my horror, a renovation had been done, and now fake wood paneling covered the wall and *the picture*. I stood there frozen, this time in disbelief. It was bad enough that the messenger was no longer and now the message?

I ran over to the bartender and did what I could to explain the significance of the picture. I was not talking to a kindred spirit; he seemed to not give a shit. I then made an offer: "I'll tell you what, I'll pay to take the wall down and put it back up. I just want to photograph that picture again." He seemed unmoved as he moved further down the bar to get far, far away from me. "Can I talk to the owner?" He suggested I come back and try to catch the owner at another time, maybe in a few months or so—very helpful, thank you.

I returned a week later: no owner, same bartender. Damn. Ok, maybe I did seem a bit wacky. Let's see if being more *playful* would be helpful; I asked if he thought the owner would ever consider selling the place. He was having more fun with this as I began to throw large *Monopoly* numbers at him.

Chez Jay is in Santa Monica on Ocean Blvd. It is a prime location surrounded by luxury housing, hotels, and restaurants. Even with the last number I tossed out, it would probably not come close to **the number**; assuming that the place would ever be up for sale.

I finished my drink and left this time with a phone number where I *might* be able to catch the owner. Just having that number in my pocket seemed to quiet my mind and the need to excavate that sign at least for a while. Plus, I knew my request was on the border of *Totallyweirdassville*.

Another two years passed, and truth be told, that picture was still on my mind. I went back and found a new bartender who seemed to have more understanding and compassion upon hearing my little story. This time, I didn't ask to buy the place or to have any walls ripped down. I just wanted to chat with the owner. He gave me the owner's card with an email address and encouraged that I connect with him. The owner's name was Mike.

I emailed Mike and we planned a meeting. My rendez-vous came on December 13, 2013. I was there early and noticed that since I had been there, Chez Jay was given landmark status. Good. Would we need special permits from the City of Santa Monica to take down a thin ply-wood wall? If the Santa Monica Landmark Preservation of-fice were anything like the traffic and parking enforcement office, or if my name were to be mentioned . . .

Mercifully, in walked Mike to stop the buzz in my head. I told him my story acknowledging how crazy it may have seemed (and still might). He understood, and then he be-gan to tell his story. This was his home; he had taken it over after Jay had passed. He spoke of Jay as being a larger than life character much like my brother. He was open to my re-quest of taking the wall down but seemed skeptical that the picture would be found. We continued to exchange stories. I asked him to take a closer look at the picture on my iP-hone. All of a sudden, a light went off: long before iPhones, there had been a phone booth in that spot and inside on the wall stood my sacred painting. Now, he knew exactly where it was.

Mike asked for me to send him a picture of my brother

and to give him a week to consider my request. Mike needed to connect with the man who did the renovation.

I left feeling optimistic.

As promised, a week later, I received a very nice email from Mike. He recognized my Mike. Sadly, however, the part of the wall with the painting on it had been removed and discarded when they completed the renovation. Even though it was not the conclusion that I wanted, I fully accepted it very aware that we don't always get the endings we want. I was grateful to *Chez Mike* for going out of his way to be so kind.

As I close my eyes and imagine that old building forever set against a big blue Santa Monica sky with all the new buildings that now surrounded it, I realize it's not *where* it lives that matters, it's *that* it lives . . .

And that's my final answer.

Dedication

To: my/our mother and father who managed to come together for enough time to give me/us life.

To: my grandmother who modeled how to live one.

To: my twin.

To: my husband who gave to me the wind, the sand, and the stars in the form of two little people.

To: my two little people, so proud and grateful to be your mommy.

To: all of my very dear friends and family.

To: Audra, the saint on my imaginary medallion.

To: the teacher who patiently taught me to read. Her name was Faith. Whenever I was struggling she would say to me: "What's my name?" and I would answer, "Faith" and then she would reply: "That's right, always remember, have faith," and so I did.

To: all of those mentioned (and not) within who bumped into me along the way and helped to fill the pages of my life.

Acknowledgements

This is where the "*but for*" rule is in full force and effect. *But for* the following people, I would have never written this (blame them):

Alex: my firstborn. While we walked around her college campus and discussed her future, I told her a story about my past. At its conclusion she said, "Wow, you really need to write that." I quickly launched into a million reasons why I couldn't. She then rolled her eyes and said, "If I said that to you . . ."

Laura: a dear friend who works for a big film studio and has produced many films. After telling her the story of my experience at the medical marijuana dispensary, she responded, "You know, I've never seen that scene written anywhere; why don't you write it?" Visiting the Pot Apothecary was the first story I wrote. To make certain that I was not embarrassing myself (too much), I made her read every other story and many drafts of each until her inbox threw-up, and I developed the discipline and courage to go forward on my own.

Diana: a dear friend who has made scores of films including four or five of my own. She too was subjected to many of my early drafts. Diana is a *no bullshit* professional who once threw me off of my own film set for allegedly having distracted the director. I counted on her honest evaluation of this material. As with Laura, I appreciated her encouragement and her wise notes. Both helped to push my lazy ass forward.

Gena, Pam, Sue, Robin, Debbie, and so many of my Vixens: all dear friends and all very smart opinionated women who would tell me if my hair color was not right or my outfit was inappropriate . . . and all subjected to my whining insecurities and early drafts. All put fuel in my tank.

Christine: my young, smart, talented friend. Christine edited this opus. She is the person most responsible for making me look much smarter than I actually am. I was lost in a dizzying array of semicolons, colons, commas, dashes, and slashes—all of which gave me a terrible headache. She made all of the corrections, sprinkled clarity when needed and patiently explained many grammar rules, some of which I may even remember. If not, and should I ever attempt additional writing, I will continue to rely upon her skill and intelligence (a smart decision on my part).

Naomi & Marija: Very professional publishing and graphic design services thanks to these two women.

AND FINALLY:

Alva: the ICU nurse who took such good care of my brother after his brain biopsy. She was known for making homemade applesauce for her favorite patients. Mike ate a lot of applesauce. Whenever he'd ask, "How'm I doin?" she'd reply, "Mike, you're on the Okey Dokey Trail."

On my brother's headstone it reads: *Forever on the Okey Dokey Trail.*

Made in the USA
San Bernardino, CA
27 September 2014